Lot 84

With Powder on My Nose

With Powder

Billie Burke

Coward-McCann, Inc.
New York

on My Nose

WITH CAMERON SHIPP

Illustrations by Vasiliu

For

Marjorie Merriweather Post May

Contents

Contents
❧ 8

With Powder on My Nose

Chapter 1

WITH POWDER ON MY NOSE

IT SEEMS to me that Introductions to books are like introductions at cocktail parties—nobody ever pays any attention to them. But sometimes you wonder who your hostess is.

Billie Burke is my real name, not a stage name. I was named for my father, Billy Burke, who was a singing clown with Barnum & Bailey and in Europe many years ago. I was formally baptized "Mary William Ethelbert Appleton Burke" in Westminster Abbey, London, a name immediately ignored by everybody. Since I started on the stage in England some people believe I am English. I'm thoroughly American, born in Washington, D.C. My mother's family was from New Orleans and my father's from Ireland.

Legally, on formal invitations, and always in my heart, I am Mrs. Florenz Ziegfeld, Jr.

There is one other confusion about who I am that I'd like to clear up. Whenever I do a play or a picture, or appear on television, I meet people or get letters from people who remember me in the *Ziegfeld Follies* of 1914. The ladies—some of them my age—tell me that their nurses took them. The men were all sophomores at Princeton. So far as the year goes, this could be true; and the idea is flattering because all Ziegfeld Girls were famous beauties. But I was not one of them. I was an actress on Broadway in my own plays and I became Mr. Ziegfeld's wife, not one of the Girls.

Most people call me "Billie" or "Miss Burke." Today, if you are an actress, a ballplayer, a neighbor, or President of the United States, you are called by your first name or nickname as a matter of course. In Paris in the eighteenth century it was considered good manners for men to kiss actresses on the neck when they were introduced. I like informality but I do not go quite that far back.

In my small house in West Los Angeles and in the garden outside my sitting-room window—where I am looking now, distracted by the ballet-fluttering of a pale-blossoming apple tree and by the juvenile advances of a wisteria vine which is determined to embrace everything—in my small house and garden there are a number of little elephants.

They are an inch or so to a foot and a half high. They are made of china, crystal, porcelain, amber, silver, gold, and jade. In the garden near the tree is a large porcelain fellow from Dives, France, where they also make china cats which hang from roofs and cling to chimneys.

The elephants belonged to my husband, who collected them all his life. They hold their trunks high, symbolizing good luck. Once when my daughter Patricia was a child in Hastings, New York, Flo brought her a small live elephant for a plaything. Flo thought nothing of that. He was likely to bring home anything, from a pocketful of diamonds (he did that several times) to twenty guests for dinner.

My sitting room here is small and cluttered. Paul Crabtree, who wrote and produced *Lady of the House*, the play I did in Palm Beach last year, walked in one day and said, "Billie, this scene doesn't just happen. I'm convinced that you have a property man come in every morning and set your stage."

I don't. I don't even have a maid. I make my own clutter. If it seems actressy, the fact is that I can put a finger on anything I want instantly—with more efficiency than if I had baffling cross indexes and steel cabinets. My desk spills over with television scripts, water colors by grandchildren, and cards from old friends pretending that birthdays are fun. And clippings. I find something fasci-

nating to clip every day to send on to someone or to keep on my desk and wonder why I clipped it.

Over there on the wall, slightly tilted, is a picture of an elegant young man. He wears a frock coat, a bat-wing collar, and a tall hat. He has an ascetic face and a military mustache. This is a photograph of Somerset Maugham, who today reminds everybody that he is "a very old party," of eighty-four. I prefer to be reminded of him by this photograph taken when he was about thirty—this helps me feel younger. Photographs of Bernard Baruch and Booth Tarkington are also askew. This is because they are part of my filing system. I keep putting notes behind them.

(One of the notes says: *Remember to write about the mother-in-law who owns a yacht.* An attractive idea. I wonder what I meant.)

Will Rogers' chaps from a *Follies* show hang over there next to the bronze bust of Flo Ziegfeld. Behind these are the white gloves Eddie Cantor wore in *Whoopee!* On the walls are playbills of the *Ziegfeld Follies* of 1914 and 1917 and other wonderful years. And wherever possible there are pictures of me.

This is one of the advantages of being an actress. You can put up all the pictures you want of your favorite actress without being considered immodest. If someone asks who your favorite actress is, you can always say "Helen Hayes," unless you happen to be Helen Hayes.

This is not my first book. The first one was my auto-biography, *With a Feather on My Nose*, published ten years ago. As I glance through it now I find that I would make no changes in it; it is the true story of a redheaded actress who was a light comedienne and who was in love. It does not—quite properly—say the troublesome, criti-

cal, serious things about women which need to be said
today.

For a few weeks after *Feather* came out, I left copies
around the house where I thought they would be exposed to the greatest flow of guest traffic and influence
people to go to the bookstore and buy it. I discovered an
odd thing: Strangers would pay money for it (we had
a good sale and I am still comforted by small royalties)
but friends who could buy *me* wouldn't buy my book.
They expected to get it for nothing, especially the rich.

They would pick up one of my books and say, "Billie,
autograph this, will you? Write something cute."

I'd grimly write something cute: *For Gert, who knows
and understands the Ubangis,* or *For Charles, who inadvertently stuck this literature in his pocket.*

Now I know better. If you are reading this book you
paid for it, or the library did, or a friend did, or you had
to have a birthday or an operation to get it for a present.
Somebody bought it.

As an Author—an exciting new role for me and I
played it to the hilt—I made the usual number of talks to
literary club ladies in which we looked over each other's
hats and they wondered how old I was. I went to stores
in New York, Chicago, Detroit, Brooklyn, San Francisco, and a number of other cities. I autographed fly-
leaves with deep gratitude, counting the profits. And I
overheard something.

I overheard it, in various ways, a number of times, but it was summed up one rainy afternoon in a crowded Chicago department store when one woman said to another:

"I saw her in a play in nineteen-*seven*—and she was no child then—but right now she doesn't look a day over forty!"

Dear overheard lady, may the saints keep you! I was rather past forty when you said that but I was "on"—I was acting. I had in mind a sophisticated, half-past-soubrette but definitely not aging type of actress—to be exact, Cornelia Otis Skinner. If I underplayed by ten years, I haven't a regret in the world. I am convinced that every woman should consider herself "on" wherever she is—in a steaming kitchen, in a bedroom, or behind the footlights. She should at all times put her best foot forward. That is, if her foot is her best feature. If not, put something else forward.

I am going to say that it is the responsibility of all women, the actresses, the unwed, the wives, the mothers, the grandmothers and the mothers-in-law, to know themselves as women, to rejoice in it, and to *be women in every possible way.*

This isn't as simple a statement as it may seem. It is plain to me, and it must be plain to every person who reads magazines, or who moves in any circle from junior executive suburban to society and saloons, that American women are disturbed. They are in revolt.

They are disturbed by their natural roles in the animal kingdom. They are actually in revolt against being women.

And I believe that this is God's world. If you concede that this is likely, then it must be that we are all here for a reason. The only possible reason, in God's world, is Love.

If women are not made for love, as the main treasurers and inspirers of love, then there is no reason for them. It can hardly be that we are on hand merely to cook and clean. Certainly it doesn't make much sense to consider that we're here to compete with men. (*For* men perhaps, not with them.)

In my simple way I approach these thoughts as practically as I can. To be a woman, it seems to me, is a responsibility which means giving, understanding, bearing, and loving. To begin with, these things require being as attractive as possible.

I try. As for age, I am pleased but not overwhelmed when people tell me that I don't look mine. I don't and I darn well know it. This is no accident. I have worked at it for years.

There is one more thing to say about me.

When I was very young I acted in plays by Somerset

Maugham, Booth Tarkington, Sir James M. Barrie, Sir Arthur Wing Pinero, and Alexander Dumas. These were light, smart comedies. I was an ingénue, dressed in high fashion. (My clothes were very important; they were the main reason for my early successes.)

I was amusing on stage because I had delightful costumes, because I had witty lines to say, written by the wittiest authors, and because I worked.

As Mack Sennett used to say, "My comedy is no laughing matter." I rehearsed and toiled as hard as I could to get the effects my directors and my authors wanted.

Naturally, many persons associated the sophisticated girl on the stage with me. Of course, I was never that girl at all: I *acted* her.

Later, when I went into motion pictures, I played spoony ladies with bird-foolish voices. These women were not me, either. I had to create them.

I played the skitter-wits so long in Hollywood that, alas, I am "typed." I discover all the time that I am more famous than I think I am—for being silly. Now, out of force of habit and because it is expected of me, I catch myself unnecessarily creating the impression that I am irrational. It's not difficult. I'm good at it.

But the notes that I mentioned earlier (behind the pictures) are serious. Women are not always as funny as they seem, even me.

James Branch Cabell wrote a terrifying line in one of

his books. He said, "Women see with bright and horrible eyes."

I assume that Mr. Cabell meant that women are realistic. They have to be realistic, far more than men. All the dirty little jobs and all the intimate, immediate facts of birth and death are women's concerns. Men flee from these things to become engineers or dry-goods merchants, or to write sonatas. Men have a lot more time to write sonatas, which is often hard to do if you are changing a baby or having one.

I want to get down to simple cases and tell what I know and I hope I don't have a mishap. If I get accidentally intellectual, you won't believe it's me, and neither will I.

But we have to talk about critical things. There are older women, for instance, whose problems are just brushed aside—the way *they* are brushed aside. Their helplessness and loneliness and the love that goes to waste or turns bitter are American tragedies.

To be honest, it's often their own fault. There are positive things they can do to be better and to live better.

I think women all over are distracted and in revolt for a handful of reasons:

Some women have forgotten how, or never learned, or resisted learning, how to be true women.

Too many think they have to prove they are as good

as men by competing with them. Win or lose the competition, they are jealous of men.

Many, regardless of age, are lonely.

They are getting old.

As wives and mothers, they do not respect their work
in their homes or respect themselves for doing it.

Older women become frantic about their looks and
make ghastly mistakes in make-up and dress.

Or they are mothers-in-law.

I don't find myself everywhere on that list, as you
don't either, but I can add some special complaints of my
own. I'd prefer to be younger; I live alone; I have been
a widow for eighteen years and I miss—at times desperately—the husband I loved, the touch of his hands, the
sound of his step; I had to fight to keep that man (I fought
in panic, but I am so very glad I did); I am not well off;
and I am one of the victims of America's favorite joke, a
mother-in-law.

There's another worry that sometimes makes witches
out of actresses and, goodness knows, many other women
who aren't actresses. This is the getting-on-in-years bit
by ex-honeypots. Either they really were honeypots or
now in their latter days they have decided they were—
there being nobody around to tell on them. Some of
these gals are mournful, as if the clock should have been
stopped just for them. Some, whether they were honeys
or not thirty or forty years ago, have a natural instinct

for dress and make-up which makes them look nice, dear, or smart. Then there are the poor things who turn up in rigs with faces powdered purple.

I have some words for all of you, and they are not all my words. I've consulted some authorities.

As for me, sister, I have no time to pout by the fireplace about how marvelous I think I used to be. For an old girl I'm in darn good shape right now and I'll tell you how I've kept that way.

Chapter 2

THE TROUBLE WITH WOMEN

I ALWAYS SAID the right things about love and marriage when I was on the stage. That was because I said what good playwrights wrote for me to say. I often said the wrong things to my husband.

One time I said so many wrong things in an argument and he replied with so many exasperating, unanswerable things that I had to throw a silver soup tureen at his head.

This had a certain theatrical effect. (A brick would not have done. Always fling something expensive.) There are times when the only possible way to deal with some husbands is to throw at them.

We wound up in laughter.

After all, there are no absolute rules about how to be a woman and cope with men. We have to make up our axioms as we go along. Then we can change them. Just don't let men invent rules at you first. They *won't* change.

Dale Carnegie, who wrote *How to Win Friends and Influence People*, the most accurate book I know of about human relations, and full of fine rules, said privately that there are times when the only way to handle a situation is to cut loose—throw something.

Up to the time I began reading and clipping from newspapers and magazines, I thought there was nothing wrong with women that Slenderella couldn't fix.

Now when I pick up an article about women I don't know whether I'm reading science fiction or a horror story. I agree with Inez Robb, who wrote in her column recently: "I can remember 'way back ten or fifteen years ago when I was as relaxed as a ragged mop and as loose as a goose."

But now, Inez says she's "tense, jittery, as wary as a canary, and so nervous I could scream." She thinks she might scream.

This is because Miss Robb has been "prodded, poked, thumped, dissected, bisected, and burped. I have been viewed with alarm, affection, despair, dislike, delight,

antipathy, distaste and witchery. As an American woman
I have been described as a mess, a mouse, a monster, a
maladjusted mom, and a marked-down Marilyn Monroe.
... I am confused. Which periodical do you read?"

Inez and I must have been reading the same magazines.
(There was one book I didn't read, by Marynia Farn-
ham and Ferdinand Lundberg, called *Modern Woman:
The Lost Sex*. I've been pushed pretty far but I decline
to get lost.)

Anyway, *something's* wrong or all these article writers and researchers wouldn't be so vehement about women. Even a lady anthropologist takes off agin us. Dr. Margaret Mead comes up with the statement that more than a quarter of a million women in the United States are "articulately and definitely disturbed about their lot as women."

There's a bit more to it than this. Statistics bore you? Me, too. But you may not know what terrible shape you're *in*:

For instance, 27 million women had jobs in 1955. That was about 30 per cent of all the working people in America. You'd think men never had it so easy with so many females toiling to support themselves, but ah, no—the working girl is not a happy little breadwinner; she's a problem.

Merle Miller (he's a novelist and they figure things out) says, "They are almost all insecure and neurotic, out of place in the business world and ill at ease at home. In allowing the feminists to persuade them that they should become second-rate men, they have given up every chance of becoming first-rate women."

This is a point. Everybody knows executive-type career girls who push too hard even when they do two men's work. But most working women are not competing with men to be Vice-President, although they may be competing with each other to be Mrs. Vice-President.

Now I find a complaint against women that I can't try to explain away. They drink too much. The number of female alcoholics jumped from 376,000 in 1940 to 710,-000 in 1955. That's what the Yale University Center of Alcoholic Studies says. (They have some way of keeping track of tippling women. Must be fascinating.)

We might toss that statistic off hardheartedly by saying, "Be kind to the old bowsers, boys, and buy 'em another gin at the bar," but these drinking women aren't old bowsers. When men become alcoholics, they seem to put in full time at it. Most of them don't have time to get married. The more the women drink, the more marriage-minded they get. How they do it I don't know, but girls with a high alcoholic content attract men and marry them one after another. Of course, they run the divorce rate up, according to Yale. Here it is: The divorce rate among drinkers is 32 times the divorce rate of abstainers.

As I read on, though, I gather that the main trouble with being a woman is not alcoholism (Is your neighborhood full of drunk wives and sober husbands?) or office work (Are the majority of working girls little monsters?) but a revolt among women themselves *against being women.*

There's conflict between the husband and the housewife because she resents the limitations of her job. She wants to be "equal" but at the same time she wants to be feminine.

She isn't upset because she doesn't get her hands on the money. Wives control more than 60 per cent of every dollar that's spent in the United States, and 51.6 per cent of all the stock in Wall Street is owned by women.

There's more, but that's all the percentages and statistics I can bear, proving that I am a mess. 'Tain't necessarily so.

Chapter 3

KITCHEN, BEDROOM, AND BATH

WHEN I WAS first married I fell in love with my husband every night.

Flo would emerge from his bathroom immaculate, hair brushed soft and clean, in white linen pajamas buttoned at the top of the shoulder, with a small, up-turned collar like those the Russians wear. He loved bath powder and cologne, which he imported from Paris. And it was always like this, for eighteen years, no matter how late he got home at night. I just couldn't believe that I'd married such a fascinating man.

I know—you're going to point out that Florenz Ziegfeld, Jr., had a great deal of money and could afford these things. Also, that there are many marriageable gents who would prefer to smell like saddle soap, or a football team locker room—anything—rather than cologne from Paris.

All right.

But there are mighty few men worth seeing more than once, let alone sharing a bed with, who can't put up with hot water and soap.

I tell you this: Clean linen, brushed hair, showers, soap and water add considerably to the bliss of married life. I'm constantly amazed when I talk to young people— they are frank and tell everything—to learn how much they know about Sex and how little about soap.

Let's suppose that you are the feminine half of a married couple with small, loud, reluctant children to get off to school in the morning. And, of course, a husband to feed and send out to cope the best he can in the jungle called Business.

It's an explosive scene, usually. "Who stole my algebra book?" Small boys are always convinced that their relatives are thieves in regard to algebra books. "Where's my shirt?" This is standard. No man can *see* a shirt. You have to *hand* it to him. "For God's sake, get out of the bathroom! I'm late." Architects are idiots. They should make all bathrooms bigger than living rooms, accommodating at least six children—or they should put in six little bathrooms.

In this pre- and post-breakfast pandemonium of small and large kinfolk suffering from the shock of cold water after warm beds, the lady of the house is supposed to be cook, psychiatrist, detective, laundress, valet, traffic cop, and plumber. That's her job, and if she doesn't do it efficiently she can start all her people off to a bad day, or give them dreadful complexes, or at least heartburn. Too many times the poor thing does her chores well but forgets herself. She flaps around in flannel, run-down slippers, and a hairdo that resembles a nest clawed together by an alarmed bird in a hurry to lay an egg. It's a mistake, girl. You're neglecting the most important ingredient of marriage—namely, YOU. But you can do something about it, and this isn't as difficult as you might think.

It's your job to creep out of bed early—ten minutes early will do it, five in a pinch—get scrubbed (or *look* scrubbed), brush your hair and your teeth, put on something crisp, use some scent, and—no matter how tired you are, no matter how your head aches, no matter how late you were up last night—*look kissable!*

Rule: Don't dare, ever, to get caught in the morning with messy hair or with last night's stale rouge on your mouth.

This morning ritual is not something I have just invented and want to try out on you. I know about this

Vasiliu

because I practiced it for many years. Now that I don't have to do it for the same reasons you do, I continue it for my own reasons: I feel better, the day starts fresher, people like me better, even if the people today are only the paper boy or the milkman.

When Flo and I lived in the big house at Hastings, outside of New York, we had those comforting things now associated with the tax-exempt past: servants, money, and time. I was an actress. I did not have to rise at dawn. I could have breakfast in bed, and breakfast could be as late as I wanted it to be.

But I took care to awaken first, before my husband popped an eye at me. I would get gently out of bed, steal to the bathroom, and do a wash-polish-brush-scent job on myself. Then I would creep back into bed and pretend to be asleep.

When my husband awakened and looked at me— the first thing a husband sees in the morning, whether he likes it or not, is *you*—I'd be at my best.

I'll admit I had unusual inspiration for setting my stage as well as I could. When my husband left for work, he left to work with the *Ziegfeld Follies* Girls.

More than likely your husband doesn't leave home to work with chorus girls. At least, not every day. But hear this: When he goes to his store, his laboratory, his office, or his factory, or on his sales rounds, he constantly meets young women who are as attractive as any professional beauties who ever wiggled before the footlights. These are the tidy, fresh, scrubbed business girls.

Perhaps, before you were married, you used to be one. Then you'd know. These are about the most fetching young women on view anywhere in the world. They share interests, problems, and coffee breaks with your boy—and he's with 'em at least eight hours a day. That's often more than you have him, awake.

Don't give him a chance to make unfortunate comparisons.

Get *out* of that bed. A few gallons of hot-and-cold water in the shower will do you more good than "beauty sleep"—which will only make you look more rumpled.

It takes only five minutes!

There's nothing so discouraging to a husband as a wife who constantly looks hot in the face and whose hair looks as if an eagle slept in it. I'm saying this: Always look accessible, morning, noon, and night. This can be done any time of day even if you have just emerged from cleaning the doghouse.

Of course you have to work fast and sometimes in secret so that demanding fellow doesn't see the magic you create for his sensitive eyes and nostrils. Never use heavy perfumes. Horrible!

Lady Duff Gordon, sister of Elinor Glyn who wrote *Three Weeks* and called Clara Bow the "It" girl, used to say a good thing. She said that "the sweet freshness of nighties, dressing gowns, blouses, and morning coats should always make a man want to know the wearer a little better."

It seems to me, after studying the statistics until my eyes blur, that the sociologists and the attorneys and Yale

University have all said true things about the causes of divorce. But one of the main reasons for divorce isn't a statistic yet. It's *sloppy women.*

Men will stick to fat ones, skinny ones, old ones, and forked-tongued ones. We all know that. But they won't cling to gals who are messes.

And: It seems to me that married people should be at least as painstaking personally before they go to bed as they are before they go out to dinner.

I studied the Ziegfeld Girls, and I listened to what Flo Ziegfeld said about them. Under the circumstances, I considered it part of my job to hold my husband—and this was not exactly a part-time job.

There were two notable things about Ziegfeld Girls. I recall that Flo and Cecil Beaton, the British designer and photographer, had a shouting argument about the shape of things in girls. Mr. Beaton seemed to believe that a straight line is the shortest distance to appeal and favored flat-chested women. Mr. Ziegfeld, and most other men, never believed that. He starred voluptuous girls—it never occurred to him to glorify anything boy-like. But some of the most attractive *Follies* beauties did not have enormous bosoms. He admitted that there was attraction in the "small but perfect," a phrase he liked.

This argument between Ziegfeld and Beaton took

place more than thirty years ago. It's now academic. If there ever was any doubt, the Italian girls in American movies have emphatically dispelled it.

So the Ziegfeld Girls had figures. The other feature that made them so notable was their complexions.

Every Ziegfeld Girl I ever saw, and I saw them all with jealous eyes, had complexions of peaches and cream. They had naturally pink, moist lips. Remember, in those days a complexion had to come with the girl, not from Rexall or Miss Arden. There was little more than powder to resort to, none of the thick creams that we plaster ourselves with today. And no lip rouge.

When Mr. Ziegfeld sat in his theater and had the girls pass before him on stage, making his choices for the *Follies,* he never allowed a girl to go on with powder or rouge. He'd say:

"I'd like to see you again. You have many of the requirements we're looking for, dear, but go away and wash your face and let's see what you really look like."

Even on stage myself I recall that we used as little artificial stuff as possible. Just enough to look right with stage lighting. I used no rouge off stage until I was about thirty, up until the time I was married! It wasn't respectable. Perhaps your mother recalls a horrified phrase that damned many a girl: "She *paints*!" This meant that she was "fast."

My point is that "The Great Glorifier" chose healthy girls instead of synthetic beauties.

One time, and I recall it very well, he was in Philadelphia and needed more girls for his show. He gathered them in the simplest way possible. He ignored model agencies, and the little friends of the assistant stage manager, and called in a number of secretaries for interviews. They knew nothing about the tricks of the theater, had never dreamed of becoming Ziegfeld Girls, but more than a dozen of them did—although, to be truthful, a number of them decided to stay as pretty as they were without going on the stage. The point is, of course, that you don't need a bucket of mascara, or influence, or technical training. To be attractive the main thing is to be a girl and to know it.

I thought my own taste was good, even though I usually kept it to myself and looked at my husband's beauties with green eyes. Once in the Plaza Hotel I saw a lovely girl on the elevator, spoke to her in the lobby, and asked her if perhaps she'd like to be in Flo Ziegfeld's *Follies*. I *did* have a good eye—her name was Janet Gaynor. (Never in the *Follies*. But she could have starred with Flo.)

Of all the charming girls I saw and knew, I think that Maxine Elliott was the most beautiful. Maxine was glorious all the way: teeth, hair, mouth, eyebrows—and no lipstick. The richest beaus and playboys

in the world gathered around her. She was, I'd say, better-looking than Lillian Russell, whose shape and starry blue eyes were so lovely. But Maxine was more vivid, more striking.

If you want to know what this really famous beauty was like, take a look at Ava Gardner today. I used to sit next to Ava in the Metro-Goldwyn-Mayer make-up department and marvel at that clear complexion; you could hardly believe that such beauty was real.

During my whole married life I was jealous of every woman in the *Ziegfeld Follies* and I had every right to be. The *Follies* contained, among other attractions, the dancing star Marilyn Miller. Marilyn was small, blond and exquisite, so effortlessly charming that I can understand how my husband, and every other man who had a chance, fell in love with her. But authentic Golden Girls are rare chicks. The average woman does not have to compete with them. She does have to compete with certain others, always. These cuties, whether they be wives of junior executives in the suburbs, or ladies of the chorus, or comptometer operators, have a characteristic in common.

They are playthings.

Their attraction is animal magnetism. This is all they have and they know it. They don't need anything else except to advertise their availability. Men like that. They enjoy competing for an unmoral woman out of vanity and out of curiosity. Get this ancient fact through your hard little head, please, and accept it: Even the most tepid male is often capable of being interested sexually in more than one woman at a time. He may be a shy guy and his morals may even be stuffy, but he *can* have a physical accident or a fluffy adventure without scarring his conscience and without feeling that he has betrayed the woman he really loves. Sometimes an insecure man seems to need the reassurance that he can still tumble a pretty girl. He may be scared but he'll make some kind of a fumbling try.

Women too need reassurance that they are desirable, but fortunately a noncommittal pass, a tentative insult, a whistle, or even a speculative glance are usually enough to bolster the ego. Men, the boobs, always suspect their own powers and think they have to prove them.

I think this is one of the chief reasons so many of them are capable of having affairs with two women at the same time—their wives and their playthings—without feeling guilty. Indeed, if their timing is good, they find the situation delightful so long as they are not caught or threatened.

Which is to say that *physical* infidelity may not be infidelity at all. It may be no more than an accident. You don't, of course, let the hooky-playing rascal get away with it, but at the same time you don't let nonsense break up your home, your marriage and your family.

The dog may stray (and more do than you may think), but the very last thing he wants is a smashup. You can lead straight into that by weeping, quarreling, nagging, and accusing—and that is not the proper technique for taking a plaything away from a grown man.

Don't react in hurt anger and dismay. Do this:

Act as if you don't know what's going on. Expose him to the alleged lady as often as possible—on your stage, not on hers. Have her husband around as much as possible. If she has no husband, have other men around and give her her head. If she's questionable, she'll reveal her hand sooner or later and embarrass your bemused boy. Present her with every chance to laugh too loud, sing off key, and fall on her face. You might be inspired to give her a delicate shove.

In one such instance I know of, a determined wife discovered that the plaything adored Martinis. Our girl learned to make the best—six to one, I believe was her ratio—had a party, invited the best people, including her husband's boss, and was a generous hostess. The plaything wound up being ill in a geranium bed and the hostess was very kind to her. She thoughtfully escorted her to the bathroom and revived her in a cold shower with all her clothes on.

This was a piece of low cunning. I am against alcohol.

I would not recommend anything like it without first counting to two.

In any event, don't show anger too fast. Young women tend either to explode too soon in shrill wrath or to resort to an old and worthless female trick called fighting fire with fire. They bridle and say to themselves, "I'll show *him*. If he can play around, so can I."

This is a pitiful mistake. The poor devil you choose as your fire-fighting partner will either be a heel or a poor actor or both. You'll get nowhere. And if you do make your husband jealous, you still haven't won.

Your gambit is to be so good to come home to. Be gay. Right here, of course, you want to reply, "That's easy to say and impossible to do." Let me remind you that you were gay and charming a great many times when your head ached, when your back hurt, even when you were miserable and bored and worried—before marriage.

Make everything at home, especially yourself, twice as charming as ever before. *This alone won't win for you.* This merely sets your stage, on which you have all the advantages.

If your boy doesn't come to his senses, then you decide whether he's worth keeping and whether to have a showdown. When you have that showdown, if you must, lay your cards on the table calmly—they are all trumps. Put it up to your fellow simply. He may have had it by now, you know; he may have a hurting conscience (men do have them), and he may welcome a chance to make a decision.

Ask him what he really wants. Point out what a divorce would mean. Ask him what he thinks is best for the children. If you are sure that what he wants is you and his home, you will win. If you give way to jealousy, anger, and phrase-making, you stand a good chance of losing.

I went through this years ago.

It isn't every woman's life that you can lay out and plow into as if it were in the public domain, but I can hardly claim invasion of privacy. I was married for eighteen years to a great and highly publicized show-business figure who never made small gestures. His successes, his failures, and his flirtations were matters of public interest and record, like the weather. His life became a motion picture, *The Great Ziegfeld*, made in 1936 by M-G-M.

I could not bear to see it then. No movie, and not anything I can write now, can recapture the gentle moments which were our real life together. But I saw *The Great Ziegfeld* on television the other night, twenty-three years later, with William Powell as Flo, Myrna Loy as me, and Luise Rainer as Anna Held, Flo's first wife. There was one scene, a family Christmas party at Hastings, which was very dear and very true, and there were delightful moments with a little girl of four—now my grown and married daughter Patricia. And it is a beautifully made picture. William Powell, with deep understanding, makes Flo Ziegfeld as real as he can be made on film.

But it is an experience, let me tell you, suddenly to see your own love affair and marriage and your husband's way with other women enacted in your own living room!

It was in this picture that Miss Rainer won an Academy Award for losing my husband. I could hardly believe it —she was much too pretty.

Under the circumstances, I might as well tell one more love story. It may be useful to some youngster in Suburbia who's wondering how to fight for her husband.

Flo became interested in a lady of distinction in Palm Beach. I cannot give her name, of course, but during the Twenties she was the most popular and the most beautiful woman in Palm Beach Society. She had been exquisitely reared in great luxury. She knew all the arts of entertainment and graciousness. Many men were in love with her.

The Palm Beach milieu was new to Flo. He was accustomed to extravagance. But the easy, magic touch of vast, casual wealth and amusement taken for granted was new to him.

He would be gone all day, playing cards, deep-sea fishing on yachts the size of theaters, with sophisticated groups of *bon vivants* who spoke their special tribal language of pleasure and indulgence.

Flo was a dark and challenging novelty in this group, a spectacular addition to their fun. It was true of course that he didn't belong, that he hadn't a tenth of the money necessary to belong, but he was the adventure and the catch of the season. When the lady made herself available, he fell in love.

Of course I did all the wrong things at first. I wept, scolded, and complained. This had the effect it always has in any situation between a man and a woman. It bored and annoyed the man, who then stayed away from home more than ever.

In the end, after several months, I stood my soldiers up and counted them.

I was convinced that Flo loved me and for a lot of reasons, and not alone because of sex. There have to be other reasons, too, for a marriage to hold. I knew that he appreciated the things I did for him, the home I made for him. Once in a time of deep trouble, when his financial world was about to collapse, he fell on his knees beside my bed and said:

"For God's sake, pray for me. I don't know how to pray."

And we had a child, a little girl.

And so one morning I said this:

"I won't try to hold you, Flo. Go now if you want to

go. I have made my own plans and I'll tell you what they are.

"First, I'll take Pat and we'll spend some time in Europe. I have made my reservations. After that I'll return to the stage. We'll sell the house at Hastings and end it all.

"This is the way we'll lay out our lives. Now—is this what you really want?"

There was no sudden capitulation. Don't expect that. Don't set yourself up for a martyr and anticipate a moment of triumph with your husband sniveling back to you.

Flo merely said something noncommittal, patted my arm, and went away. But he came back. His affair with Palm Beach was over. We knew what we wanted.

I could have lost it all, for both of us, in a quarrel, in a tantrum, or by trying to make him jealous. We dismissed the matter like the accident it was and never spoke of it again.

Chapter 4

WITH A POSSUM ON MY HEAD

My NEXT-DOOR NEIGHBORS are named Stephenson—Mr. and Mrs. William R. Stephenson and their four children, two teen-age girls, one seven-year-old girl, and a thirteen-year-old boy. The Stephensons are exhaustingly busy people. Mrs. Stephenson runs her house, chauffeurs children by the station-wagonful, and is involved in a bewildering round of PTA and Boy and Girl Scout enterprises requiring costumes, refreshments, and Band-Aids. Her husband is an architect. He goes to work. I like him but I know nothing about his business. The Stephensons ask me over to some of their parties and sometimes I go, but I know next to nothing about their social life except from peeking. Their endurance appalls me. I often think the Stephensons stay up too late.

I couldn't ask for better neighbors, though, and it is a joy to overhear the scurry and noise of their happy household. I live alone, so it is always pleasant merely to know that they are *there*. But I would not like to live *with* the Stephensons. We communicate daily, borrowing change for the paper boy, celebrating birthdays, chasing into the street to retrieve each other's dogs and cats—but the Stephensons' rhythms and decibels are not for me: I should prefer to fuss in an old ladies' home, or to sleep on a quiet plank, to living with my neighbors. In their house I would be a mother-in-law. In my own house I have status as a grandmother.

As I say, we see each other every day. There is a gate between our back yards. But except for the very young, who are likely to turn up at any time, usually via the kitchen, we observe informal formality about dropping in. We telephone first, or at least request permission by hollering over the fence. When the older Stephensons are in full happy cry with their friends, many of whom arrive in sports cars and ski boots, they can—and do —open their bar, or play their woofing and tweeting high-fi, or laugh at jokes I am not supposed to understand, without the inhibiting presence of an old lady.

I hated to use that phrase, "old lady." I don't feel like one. I am sure I don't act like one. I am not one. But interfere with the processes and problems of any generation younger than yours and you'll be considered an old lady even if you're an old man.

Especially if you're a mother-in-law.

Here is where I envy men, the only department in which I do envy them. They become fathers-of-the-bride, "Dad," "The Old Man," and "Gramps"—or most of them do eventually—but never fathers-in-law. Somehow or other they manage to avoid both the title and the implication, and there is no literature from funny papers to problem novels which damns them. "Father-in-law" is a courtesy phrase used for identification purposes only, as in introductions, and has no meaning. "Mother-in-law" has implications. It equates with "witch."

I note, with envy, that men become grandfathers with ease, with mock grumbles or laughter, frequently allow their pockets to get picked in the process, and sometimes wind up as doting baby sitters. No one accuses them of stirring a cauldron. And fathers-in-law and sons-in-law who can't stand each other usually manage a go-to-hell attitude from the start and thereafter leave each other alone. An admirable system.

The modern deal among grandfathers is to get their grandchildren to call them by their first names, a camaraderie neither mothers-in-law nor grandmothers seem to achieve very easily. I know a distinguished old gentle-man, a Superior Court judge, who has coached his grand-boys to call him "Butch." I never knew a mother-in-law called "Butch," or even "Mary Jane."

Why is there this dreadful thing about mothers-in-law?

How come an attractive, modern, intelligent, and often devoted and self-sacrificing woman becomes an automatic horror the moment her son or daughter gets married?

It's a conditioned reflex, that's what it is. It springs out of the dawn of prehistory like a racial bad dream. Our fur-bearing forefathers were against their mothers-in-law, possibly because they stole their daughters in tribal raids—or because they traded cows for them and cheated.

Or maybe because even then mothers-in-law talked too much.

Plainly, I don't know, and the scholars don't know precisely why either. But it is firmly established that the mother-in-law fetish is ancient, that we inherited it, and that we cling to it like other old superstitions, such as being afraid of the dark. If you are a MIL, it *may* not be your fault that your SIL thinks you are a lady witch doctor.

At any rate, all savages regarded their MIL's with dread. This is one of the most familiar facts of anthropology. When Sir James Frazier wrote about mothers-in-law in *The Golden Bough,* he put them in a chapter entitled "Taboo and the Perils of the Soul." I sometimes wonder what Sir James thought about *his* MIL.

The point is that the mother-in-law pattern got set a very long time ago and its traces are still evident in all tribes, from tribes of Indians to tribes of Stanford graduates.

Here is some delightful information, calculated to make the old girls feel better—at any rate important:

The Dakota Indians, the Battas of Sumatra, and the Dyaks of Sarawak were not allowed to speak to their wives' mothers or to look at them.

Among the Victorian tribes of Australia it was the custom—probably still is, and probably a good thing—for a mother-in-law to stay at least fifty yards away from her son-in-law. If she met him accidentally she had to hide her head under a rug.

And take the Gudangs of New Queensland, the Caffres of South Africa and the Nisinan tribe of California, not to mention our own Apache Indians who were alleged to be the fiercest of the fierce: They were all afraid to mention the names of their mothers-in-law. The Cape York aborigines and the Kowaregas of Prince of Wales Island did mention their MIL's, but they had to make up new names for her, which they probably did with enthusiasm.

The Kurnai tribe of Victoria had a custom which fascinates me. It would solve many a domestic problem of today. If a mother-in-law called on her son-in-law she had to cover her head with a possum rug.

That's what I read in books, cribbed it, and put it in here as a matter of interesting information. Possibly it's useful. The next time your MIL bothers you, tell her to go put a possum on her head.

My mother-in-law, Mrs. Florenz Ziegfeld, Sr., was a small, charming, fresh-and-tidy person, French in manner and extraction, who was much too dear and doll-like to upset even an anthropologist. She did upset me, once.

When Flo and I were first married she brought me her most precious possession. This was not a cascading necklace or an heirloom brooch or a favorite miniature of her son, but, of all things for me, an actress, a cookbook.

"Here, my dear," she said, "are all of Floshen's favorite dishes. He is very particular, you know, and if you wish to keep him happy—"

And she handed me an old, worn, much-used compendium of Austrian and German pastries, strudels, stews, pies and cakes which only a devoted mother or a *cordon bleu* chef could have prepared.

I was never a little hot-in-the-face bride making a burnt offering of myself over a stove to please my husband. I did not think Mr. Ziegfeld married me for a cook. I do not to this day think any man **or boy** marries a girl for a cook unless he runs a restaurant.

I had never cooked anything, not even a fried egg over a gas jet in a dressing room. But I was an actress. I read the recipes aloud, with appropriate inflections over the sauces, impressing Mrs. Ziegfeld, and promised I would nourish Floshen with all of them. I think this was one of my best performances. But I never went farther with this act than the audition. I employed the best chefs possible to feed my husband and never ventured near the kitchen. Parenthetically, I have never believed that the way to a man's heart is through his stomach. Betty Crocker is probably the most widely pictured woman in the world, but it's Jayne and Marilyn who get pinned up.

Why the tribesmen were scared of their mothers-in-law I'm not sure, as I said. The reason for mentioning them is to argue that a woman who becomes a MIL has got a good deal of historic prejudice to overcome no matter how hard she tries to be civilized. We MIL's start out as authenticated monsters. The trick is to recognize that and then do what we can about getting accepted as human beings.

Instead, alas, some of us take one or more of these points of view:

That my son's wife is—has to be—a no-good hussy who trapped my poor little boy;

That I can do everything better than my daughter, or daughter-in-law, and she's ungrateful if she doesn't let me, even when I deliberately make her look like a fool;

That I'm neglected and should let everybody know it by hint, whine, complaint, and criticism;

That a married son or daughter is like a paid-up insurance policy on which I can retire;

That I've always quarreled violently with my daughter, therefore my son-in-law should let me continue quarreling with her in his home;

That I'm a third partner to a young marriage, entitled to know everything, share all decisions, and use my SIL's charge account;

That they don't know how to bring up children, God knows, and it's up to me to show them;

That my SIL is a callow and cruel youth who will never be the man his father-in-law was;

That my thirty-five-year-old daughter with three children is still the immature daughter she was when she married at twenty;

That mother knows best.

There are women who expect to have two husbands: their own and their daughter's. I don't understand why they think they are entitled to this, but they do. They are the ones who weep the most at weddings. I have always thought this is because they are so pointedly left out of the ceremony.

They think, these old girls do, that a son-in-law who comes from a totally different environment, who has experienced a totally different family life, should suddenly conform to them. The plain fact is that the average son-in-law is, to begin with, barely aware of his girl's mother. He doesn't know her, doesn't necessarily want to know her, feels no obligation to her—*has* no obligation to her.

Over the years I've seen many young wives painfully trying to make their young husbands adore their mothers-in-law. They argue, explain, and scold. They'd better save their breath and their tear ducts. It takes time and it takes patience for a man to get over the notion that his MIL is a bad-luck symbol better swept under a rug. Better than pleading is this approach: "Look, dear, I know the old girl drinks a little and tells lies, but she's harmless and we don't have to have her around all the time."

In this instance the protagonists were named Albert and Dorothy. Albert considered his MIL an unendurable stick, possibly a toad, up with whom not to be put. One evening when Dorothy was out getting advice from a marriage counselor, he gave her mother an experimental swig of Southern Comfort and found her quite charming, if untruthful. He and his mother-in-law were loudly watching *Maverick* when Dorothy returned. They are still conspiratorial friends but they do not see each other often. Dorothy stays home from the marriage counseling to keep them apart.

I have blazing convictions about mothers-in-law and I am not always powdering my nose when I say them. It seems to me that the most fundamental mistake most parents make with children is to expect them to be grateful.

Children are never grateful.

They are not supposed to be. They are not in debt. They do not owe you anything except what they have found in you, over the years, to love and respect; and even this they may properly take for granted. You should feel lucky if there have been incidents in your relationship which throw a strong focus on your personality, if there are recollected times of grace under pressure worth more than taking for granted.

The remembrance of the sweetness of a face, the love a son or daughter has seen in the eyes of a mother or father, are forever a joy and a solace to a child who has been brought up with sweetness and courage.

But there is no debt. Don't try to collect it like a promissory note.

The "sacrifices" you made were not for *them*, they were for *you*. If you suffered, if you truly did, then you graced your own spirit more than any other spirit and you are the winner and the debtor.

In my own case, with a doting and indulgent daughter who often thinks I am funny and a son-in-law who picks me up and teases me, I am—let's face it—extraordinarily lucky. I think the Stephensons have never seriously considered poisoning me. There have been times, and there are still times, when they wish I would shut up.

Sometimes, with great courtesy and tact, they tell me to shut up.

This is when I fuss, and, as Will Rogers used to put it, "stomp around."

I do this more than I should with the Stephenson children. Flo Ziegfeld was a man of impeccable manner and exquisite taste. He had, of course, a flamboyant heartiness but, as his professional work always revealed, he also had a taste and an instinct for elegance. He had a touch of the *grand seigneur*. In short, he had good table manners. And so—at least this is my excuse—I too often lose patience with my grandchildren and exhibit bad manners in correcting their bad manners.

I expect them to have the same *savoir-faire* that polite society with a butler behind each chair displayed in 1903. I know that Miss Emily Post is alleged to put her elbows on the table today but I blow my top when a thirteen-year-old boy who's late for school does the same thing.

Vasiliu

I am accused, too, of being psychologically illiterate. I snap "No," "Don't," and "Stoppit" at young people. They look as rugged as small horses to me, but it seems that young people today are delicately constituted in the psyche and will get a trauma or something horrid out of Professor Freud's books, if they are exposed to negatives.

As a result of being told by his grandma to get his dirty feet off her sofa and don't do it again, boy, under pain of a whacking, it seems that a young man can get an inhibition, the psychosomatic sniffles, or an Oedipus-in-law complex.

I don't know about that. I am convinced that a majority of today's young people, boys and girls, would be vastly improved in both manner and psyche by a few (I don't mean few, I mean a good many) fannie-strappings. But I can't say this anywhere except in my own book.

At any rate, the shut-up principle is the working principle, and so far as mothers-in-law and grandmas are concerned, it does work. Let's be realistic. If you want your in-laws and your grandchildren to come near you, shut up. Let them put their feet on your sofa. Let them lean their elbows on the table. It's a cheap price to pay for what you want—which is attention.

The ideal mother-in-law owns a yacht—and stays on it.

My advice to all young men is to take a good, hard, long look at every nubile girl's mother before considering marrying the girl. She may be great, but the boy may be bemused by mere health or by the flattering fact that she laughs at his lack of a sense of humor. He should consider whether he is someday willing to live with the old lady.

He should consider her tempers, disposition, hypochondria, background, morals, and bank account—not that he wants her money (though it might help) but in the hope that she owns enough General Motors to be and to feel independent. He should find out what she looks like at breakfast. Even the loveliest newlywed sometimes seems less than delectable flapping around uncurried before 9 A.M. If her mother also manages to resemble a moldy haystack he'd better flee for Devil's Island than sign legal papers committing him to two frowzy females every morning when his strength is at lowest uncoffeed ebb.

He should discover whether his prospective MIL got along, or gets along, with her own spouse. If she has made her man miserable, chances are she will be expert at distressing a son-in-law.

Any man who takes on an elderly female blind is a fool. If he examines her with at least the attention he'd give to buying a horse and finds her wanting, he has a ready-made weapon to put her down—the late John Barrymore's favorite utensil, a hat. Grab it and run, son.

As for mothers-in-law, whose attention I am mainly trying to get if they'll stop yakking and listen, pray remember these simple things.

1. Let the children have their dignity. Let them alone.

2. Your greatest difficulty will not be with your son-in-law. Let him alone and he'll let you alone. Your greatest problem will be your own married daughter. *You* let *her* alone.

3. You had, or still have, your own married life. Don't be a pig and grab for another.

4. Anybody younger than you, especially your children, is geared to a different speed, a different rhythm of life. Don't interfere with this or you'll get your bustle caught in the machinery.

5. Let them come to you. Be there, always, to help, to give, to love. What else do you want? Pay?

6. Don't live with 'em. Live alone. Live anywhere. Go away. Stay away. If you can't afford this, you may find enthusiastic support from your son-in-law.

7. Be useful. Be interested in something besides your put-upon self. Get a job. Go to church. Keep cats or take up yoga.

8. You can't time this to suit yourself, but become a

grandmother as fast as possible—then be a grandmother, never a MIL.

On numbers seven and eight I feel some more wisdom coming on. Let's have a breathing spell for a moment while I stare over the back fence to see what in the world the Stephensons are up to now.

Chapter 5

WHY I NEVER MARRIED AGAIN

WHEN MY HUSBAND died in 1932, I was making a motion picture in Hollywood, *A Bill of Divorcement*, directed by George Cukor, with Katharine Hepburn and John Barrymore. It almost seems to me now, twenty-seven years later, that I went back to work the next day. This is not quite true. There were a few intervening days, during which Will and Betty Rogers took charge of everything, including me and my small daughter, but I did return to the sound stage at once, acting the best I could in a rather difficult character part.

This seemed like a hard and bitter thing to do at the

time, almost a callous thing to do. It was not, though, a matter of "the show must go on," that falsely gallant theatrical legend which is neither true nor necessary. It was, as George Cukor and Will Rogers wisely knew, simply the best thing for me and for all of us who were concerned. I was enormously fortunate that I had a job. The woman who has just lost her husband must, at any cost, in this most distressing and painful time, find something to do—anything—so that she begins at once to carry on with usefulness and dignity.

This is one of the most difficult things in the world to do. Everyone encourages you to be weak rather than strong, to postpone decisions, or let others make decisions for you, and to become a special object expecting pity. You need sympathy and understanding, but the pity is dangerous. You can go on expecting it the rest of your life—and you may get it, the worse for you.

As I was saying, I was lucky because I had my job. I was not very brave and I did not want to work. Day after day, Ern Westmore, the make-up artist, stood by to dab my eyes and cheeks so that no one would know I had been in tears, and all the others propped me up by expecting me to know my lines and act my part. I did not go through with my role out of "artistic integrity," or because one doesn't let the show down. I did it because I had to, and it was the best thing that could have happened.

I am going to say in a moment that a woman should marry again.

If this comes in shocking bad taste to someone who is perhaps as bewildered and as near hysteria as I was in the summer of 1932, please put this aside and read it later. I did not marry again. Marrying again was for a long time an incredible and disloyal thought, and I am still lonely. I still miss, not the exciting moments, not the security, not the big home, but the gentle touch of a dear hand, which it seems to me touched me only yesterday. But that was twenty-seven years ago and I know now that it would have been better if I had married again.

There are always, of course, regrets aside from personal loss when any life ends. Each instance is special, different from all others. When ambitious, useful men go, whether they are young or old, they leave their women with unfinished, haunting dreams of what they might have accomplished, the plays they might have produced, the books they might have written, the houses they might have built, the good jobs they would have done. Flo Ziegfeld had been the greatest showman Broadway had ever known and he was far from being too old at sixty-five to make the big, colorful motion pictures he planned. He could have transferred many of his great stage properties—*Show Boat* or *Rio Rita*, for instance—to the screen. But he missed all this.

He had made enormous sums of money during his

spectacular career with the *Follies* and his other big shows. How much, do you suppose? I don't know, and neither did he. Twenty or thirty million dollars has been suggested. It would have been the most casual thing in the world for him to set aside a sum, three hundred thousand dollars, a million dollars, *three* million dollars, for his wife and child.

Such a thing never occurred to him or to me.

I suppose that in the back of her mind, no matter how unselfish a person a woman is, she is bound to think later of what might have been done for her. I know so many instances of this, including my own. It is not a thought to be ashamed of. Having been protected for years, if not by wealth at any rate by a man who loved her, a woman senses—however she tries to hide it even from herself— a feeling of being neglected when it all ends.

It isn't just the money, I find out from talking to other women. It's the lack of being *looked after*.

It turns out that if you interview a thousand widows, you will not find three whose husband has provided for his demise and her future.

Husbands ought to be more thoughtful than that? Some are, indeed. They do the best they can. But isn't it really asking too much of a man, my dears? He only married you "until death do us part." He didn't plan to be taken inopportunely, leaving you with problems you never knew existed, from plumbing to banking to in-laws and taxes and loneliness. Even if you face up to it, the approach is awkward. How to say something like this to a husband:

"Dear, you are so-and-so many years older than I am, and women outlive men of equal age by about seven years anyway, so one of these days I'll be here and you'll be gone, old fellow, and what are you going to do about it?"

Can you ask, and can he answer you, in one awkward interview, this question:

"Assuming you leave me some money, my friend, what shall I do with it, how shall I invest it, where shall I live, and do you want me to get married again?"

I'll hazard a woman can get a variety of short answers to queries like that. Such as:

"I'm not dead yet, honey, and you're already planning how to spend my money." Or:

"I thought I tasted a trace of arsenic in my coffee this morning." And:

"Look, kid, let's not be morbid. Do we have to talk about that kind of thing?"

There are intelligent men to whom you cannot say such things and get even a flip answer. You cannot bear to pose the questions and they cannot bear to hear them. These are the instances in which tact and forbearance, so much a part of true love, stand in the way of love.

But it's a prudent family that manages to bring these

matters out in the open in time. And there is help at hand
for at least part of the problem. I have the greatest respect for life insurance men. When they represent the
big, sound companies, they know how to advise and to
plan for you. If they did not do this honestly, they'd
soon be caught up with and be out of business. Be sure,
when your husband buys insurance, that you sit in on
the conference and understand exactly what is happening.

But even when insurance men, estate lawyers, investment counselors, or bankers work out good financial
plans for women, they cannot do what most women
really want: decide how they are to live after their husbands are gone. To repeat a thought I mentioned before,
so many women seem to blame their departed husbands
for not making impossible plans for them. My contribu-
tion is, hopefully, that husbands as well as wives will
read this and perhaps, after a while, and no doubt after
a few shaky starts, find a way to talk about it. But mainly
I am saying that women expect too much and should get
to thinking and acting on their own.

Really, dear girl, you may expect too much.

There are eight million widows in the United States.
More wives are outliving their husbands than ever before.
In 75 per cent of marriages ended by death, it is the wife
who survives. By the end of 1960, it says in those cold
little tables prepared by Prudential, Metropolitan, and

Equitable, there will be eight million five hundred thousand widows.

One reason for this is that men tend to marry women who are younger than they are. (We could end *that* if women waited until they were thirty-six, then married twenty-one-year-old boys, in which unthinkable event we would have fewer widows but many little husbands with Mommy Boy complexes.) But the hard fact is that women outlive men anyway. Your life expectancy as of now is seventy-three years and six months, while a man of the same age can look forward to only sixty-seven years.

That is, if the business jungle does not take him sooner.

As I read the figures (I hate figures, especially these), a woman is most likely to become a widow at around the age of fifty, and she will go on for at least twenty years, alone. Even if she is sixty-five when she loses her husband she will probably be around at least as a statistic for another fifteen to twenty years.

This is good news and bad news at the same time. If you are a woman, you are going to live a good long time, longer than men, but you are going to do it without a man of your own. Think about that.

The implication is a double threat: The woman loses her husband just as she loses her youth. Tragic and awful as it is when young people die, younger women are at least better off in one respect. I mean the obvious, which is merely that they *are* young, are sure of themselves as attractive women, and have good chances to make new lives.

But when a woman becomes a widow in middle age her wants are many and difficult. She needs emotional security and freedom from anxiety—she needs money. She needs physical health and comfort. She needs to love and be loved. She needs to believe in something—a faith, a church, God. She needs to be useful.

Except for the money, which may or may not be on hand, every one of those things is up to her, like an ultimatum. She cannot start too soon to find interests, work, friends, a life of her own. She must not take advantage of the situation and of everybody's sympathy to swallow up a young family—her son's or her daughter's—or to trap and keep a child as a husband substitute.

Think how many sad instances you yourself must know, in your own neighborhood, of women who are actually fine at heart but who have kept a daughter an old maid all her life, or have turned a son into a priss because they would not let him go!

They pretend—and they deceive themselves, too—that they want their children to go, to get married. But let one prospect approach and they respond with a great variety of gambits, from sick headaches to palpitations.

Here is where I say that a woman should marry again. Let me tell you about me.

I had three main chances and rejected them all.

There was a man, lots of money, social position, distinction, all of that, whom I had known for many years in New York and Palm Beach years before his wife and my husband died. He was a gay fellow who made interesting suggestions to all pretty women. He flirted politely with me and sometimes I flirted back—safely, at the head of my own dinner table, in my own drawing room.

When the time came that he could be serious, to my surprise he *was* serious. I saw him a lot, went out with him, enjoyed every minute with him, everything about him. He asked me to marry him.

I thought: If he approached every pretty woman while his wife was alive, he'll keep on doing it if he marries again.

So I said "no" to him.

There was a man who had millions of dollars and a cattle ranch. I liked him and I liked the millions, but when he suggested that we marry, leave Hollywood and Broadway, and live on the ranch with the cows, I couldn't see it. Perhaps I should have been more adaptable. I may not be the only woman who let a herd come between herself and a man.

My third serious chance was a famous comedian. We got on famously, too, knew the same people, liked the same people, read the same books, laughed at the same jokes. Between laughs we began to feel romantic about each other.

But this fellow was not merely a professional funnyman. He had a funny face to go along with his talent. It was a dear face, I want him to know—it still is—but distinctly comical. So in a serious moment I said to him:

"I just might like you very much indeed but, my dear, I couldn't bear to wake up in the morning and see that face of yours next to mine."

"And how, my girl, do *you* look in the morning?" he asked me.

"Gorgeous!" I said. "If you give me time."

So that little affair came to a happy ending.

Which would you have chosen, the Lothario, the cattle, or the funnyface? Would your excuses have been anything like mine?

Those were my excuses, half-believable at the time, and I offer them to friends who ask me why I never married again. The truth of course is that when you have loved one man for twenty years, when you have learned his fine qualities as well as his weaknesses and his little and big idiosyncrasies, it is not so easy to let anyone take his place. And not so easy to adapt oneself to a whole new order of things. That is really why I did not marry again—and why most women don't.

But I go along now on the theory that few marriages are one hundred per cent perfect. One or the other part-

Vasiliu

ner always sacrifices many things they wish they could have in their lives. You learn to accept this arrangement and live a fairly happy life. Few of us manage to share fifty-fifty in marriage. We learn to be content and we do well indeed if we come out on the short end of a seventy-thirty deal.

Put it another way, you're a star in the marriage game if you can bat .300 and not strike out too often.

But when it comes to a second chance, we forget the percentages and expect more than we had from a first marriage! I say, don't lose the chance to make yourself and someone else happy; you can get and give a great deal more out of life than trying to go it alone with memories, no matter how sweet those memories may be.

Don't wait too long to marry again. You won't get any prettier or more desirable as the years go by and you will get harder to get along with. There is nothing that will make you so beautiful as love—nothing! The most expensive cold creams, clothes, furs, jewels, and furniture are no substitute for a man.

I take my stand for love.

To live without having known love is the saddest affair possible, even if you love and lose. Having lost, you still have precious hours of remembrance. When the Garden of Eden was created with all its beauty, and God stopped to survey all He had put in it, He realized it was worth nothing without love. No matter what the penalty was, love had to come forth before that garden could resemble Paradise. I am sure that Adam and Eve thought their punishment was well worth bearing; certainly it was better than staying on just to admire the scenery.

And what about the widow like me who does not marry again, won't marry again, or can't marry again?

This is the lady we have to be concerned about. I have already admitted that I was lucky because I had a profession and a job. But no one, no matter how untrained she is, should collapse, give up, retire, or insert herself boldly or insidiously into the homes and affairs of her children.

To put something as harshly as possible for the sake of emphasis, you could, you know, start a good life all over again at past fifty if you had just arrived in this country with no friends and no knowledge of English. This has been done and is being done. So you are not handicapped. Indeed, you have tremendous advantages in friends, family, background, education, all of which you can use (in the best sense of "use") in new and interesting ways.

Here are some things to think about:

1. Unless it's impossible, and it seldom really is, live alone and put up with it. You don't have to like it, at

first. But you will like it, I promise you from experience, and your kin will like you for it. Live with a friend, yes, if that's agreeable, but *with* someone, not *on* someone.

2. If you can do a job, do it. I know of one woman (only one, this is a special case) who when she discovered she was "unemployable" went out and did housework by the day. This temporarily embarrassed her social-minded married daughter. But it gave a lady something to do which she did exceedingly well and made her feel independent. She achieved self-respect and new friends.

3. Become a baby sitter. This is one of my main occupations, my chance to know my grandchildren better, to have them to myself and enjoy them for long evenings. As they outgrew baby needs, I began to read aloud to them. This inspires talk, discussion, and argument, and keeps me startled, awake, and sometimes informed.

4. Become a baby sitter if you don't have grandchildren, or small kinfolk of your own. Baby-sitting agencies in every city want mature and responsible women and will pay them well.

5. Don't live alone too literally. Get out, move about, go places, of course. And don't scorn the companionship of pets. Like Lionel Barrymore, I prefer cats. We each had twenty-one at one time and I have four now and a puppy. I need, as everybody needs, something to look after besides myself. (I know a woman who keeps an

African hoot owl. Well, she says, darn it, she always wanted an African hoot owl and that's that. Good for her.)

6. Did you for years pine and complain because you didn't have the time to learn French, or Modern Art, or music, or how to cut semiprecious stones? You can do it now. The adult education classes in the Los Angeles area and elsewhere are jammed with mature men and women, some of them taking courses for credit to get the college degrees they always wanted.

7. Travel, if you can, and you probably can if you won't insist on the *tour d'argent*. There are numerous excursions, many reasonable hotels where it'll cost you little. If you suspect that your in-laws would be glad to see you go, you may be surprised to discover too that they're glad when you return.

8. Best advice of all: Throw my suggestions away and think up some of your own. But do think, do experiment, do accomplish something.

Chapter 6

IF YOU WANT TO BE AN ACTRESS . . .

DEAR MISS BURKE: I am 16½ years old and have jet black hair and five feet four and all my friends say I look like Hedy Lamarr and sing like Patti Page. I just *know* I have *talent* if I had a *chance*!!! Will you please help me I want to come to Hollywood and be in pictures and I will take any *little* part to get started so just know Miss Burke I will work hard and not be just a glamor girl if you will just introduce me around or maybe write a little note recommending me to Mr. Jerry Wald. Hoping this is not too much trouble and when you see Rock Hudson tell him I think he is the greatest . . .

Very truly yours,

MARILYN FOGARTY

And:

Dear Miss Burke:

You will think it extremely presumptuous of me to write
to you, but having admired your work on Broadway and
in motion pictures for so many years, I feel that I know you
and that I can turn to you for advice. My daughter Janet, a
junior at Goucher College this year, seems to have at least
some talents as an actress—at least, she is always called upon
to play leads in college plays and, although her dramatic
coach has warned her about the vicissitudes of the professional theater, Janet is now seriously considering making a
career of acting, directing, playwriting, or television. Her
father and I would much prefer her to finish school, settle
down, and, as we say, "marry a nice boy," but if, in spite of
our doubts, she does have real talent, we do not of course
wish to discourage her. Would you recommend that she
"try her wings" in summer stock, or should she take a course
in acting in New York? Janet is our only child and we naturally wish to do the very best possible for her. Would you
advise or discourage ...

Sincerely,

Mary Ellen James

(Mrs. J. Henry James II)

I have changed the names, but those are letters
I received recently. They are the ones, like so many
others, that touch and baffle me. Like any actress, I know
what to do about typical "fan" mail:

Dear Miss Burke: You are my favorite actress. Please send
me a large autographed picture and autograph it for "My
Dear Friend Mabel."

If there is postage in the house and I can find it (the Mabels never enclose stamps), I send a small picture autographed to *My Dear Friend Mabel,* hoping she will see my next picture.* (I seem to be in a rut about this. I keep sending out photographs taken about twenty years ago.)

Answering the other letters is a good deal more difficult. They are hopeful and sincere, no matter how foolish. What is there to say to the childish Marilyn Fogartys' and to the mothers of bright, wondering girls everywhere?

Sometimes I try to write to them, but my politest notes seem to say the same thing: "Don't bother me." Sometimes I toss the letters on my desk, hoping they will go away, but they always turn up, stuck to my Los Angeles County tax statement, which never goes away.

You have to tell them all: Finish your education, read everything, act in everything you can, get discovered where you are, and *don't* come to Hollywood.

I want to add, but I restrain myself, *don't* show up on my doorstep, dear—nothing would distress me more on my threshold than a kid from Kansas who looked like Hedy and sang like Patti. I would be tempted to drown her. There are dozens, hundreds, of beautiful young girls in Hollywood, most of them working as car hops for

* John Ford's *Captain Buffalo,* coming soon to your neighborhood theater, and don't stare at television every evening. A night out will do you good.

Bob's Big Boy Hamburger restaurants, and if things don't pick up around here soon some of us older actresses will be racing them for their jobs.

Perhaps I can say here some of the things I want to tell the very young who want to be movie stars. To begin with, don't consider Hollywood unless you have:

The ambition of a Latin-American revolutionary;

The ego of a grand opera tenor;

And the physical stamina of a cow pony.

I am not being funny. It takes these qualities to endure the rebuffs, the disappointments, and the sheer labor that go into getting to be a movie star and *staying* one. Vibrant, glowing health is one of the most important factors in motion pictures, seldom mentioned, I suppose, because it is taken for granted; but by and large Hollywood's stars are the healthiest people in the world. The cameras coldly pick up any hint of illness or weakness—but they also show off strength and inner shine.

I should have listed big talent and beauty, too? They are not always requirements. A little talent, in any field, from card playing to writing to the high trapeze to acting, is often enough to take a person a long way—if it's backed by practice and character. Sheer beauty can be as tiresome as a sentimental landscape; like sleeping pills, it's a drug on the market. Miss Bergman, Miss Gardner, and Miss Taylor, for instance, are authentic beauties, but other actresses not nearly so handsome come to mind who seem beautiful because they know how to act beautiful.

To see if I was surely right about all this, I telephoned an old friend and expert, Solly Baiano, casting director at Columbia Pictures, and Ruth Burch, who casts upwards of nine thousand acting parts (literally) in television every year. They said I was correct; let the girls either stay home and get discovered in a little theater, or go to school and study. Don't storm Hollywood.

Mr. Baiano haunts every little theater and college player group in California and wherever else he has time to travel, seeing a play every night, hopeful of making a discovery. He found Alexis Smith at Los Angeles City College (an excellent acting group there); Charlton Heston at Northwestern University in Chicago; Will Hutchins ("Sugarfoot") at UCLA; Eddie Burns, Gig Young, and June Haver at little theaters he can't even remember.

Producers, talent scouts, agents, and directors are looking for new faces all the time—but they are not looking for girls on soda fountain stools on Hollywood Boulevard. The legend that Lana Turner was thus discovered has done a great deal of harm, I'm afraid. The studios are looking for girls, and boys, who have been trained by good coaches, good schools, or good little theaters.

When I say "Don't come to Hollywood and expect to break into movies or television, go to school instead," I think then that you have a right to reply, "Very well, Miss B., but you are being both negative and vague at the same time. Exactly *where* do I go to school to learn how to act?"

There are good schools in all parts of the country. The college and university schools of drama are excellent. I can list here only the ones I know myself, with embarrassed apologies to the little theaters, schools, and teachers I have to omit. And I can offer this tip: Read *Theater Arts* magazine because it's smart and knowledgeable and publishes complete Broadway play texts.

Here's that address: Theater Arts, 208 South La Salle Street, Chicago 4; five dollars a year.

The Pasadena Playhouse in California not only puts on first-rate plays in its theater but operates a first-rate school of drama. It costs $750 a year for tuition, not including board.

Here's that address and here are some others:

Pasadena Playhouse
39 South El Molino Avenue
Pasadena 1, California

Los Angeles City College   (Very fine.)
855 North Vermont Avenue
Los Angeles, California

Players Ring Theater   (Limited enrollment.)
8351 Santa Monica Boulevard
Hollywood 46, California

Falcon Studios
5526 Hollywood Boulevard
Hollywood, California

Josephine Dillon   (There are many fine
12746 Landale Street   coaches. They charge
North Hollywood, California   from $20 a week to $20
                                  an hour.)

Robert Paris
1919 Argyle Avenue
Hollywood, California

Lester Luther
7021 Hollywood Boulevard
Hollywood 28, California

Florence Cunningham
605 North Walden Drive
Beverly Hills, California

And east of Hollywood:

American Theater Wing   (Helen Hayes, president.)
351 West 84th Street
New York 22, New York

Neighborhood Playhouse   (Very famous.)
340 East 54th Street
New York 22, New York

Provincetown Playhouse   (Down Greenwich Village
133 MacDougal Street   way.)
New York City

Actors Studio   (*The* Method, with Lee
432 West 44th Street   Strasberg and Elia
New York 36, New York   Kazan.)

Boston University School of
   Fine and Applied Arts
266 Huntington Avenue
Boston, Massachusetts

Cleveland Playhouse
2040 86th Street
Cleveland 6, Ohio

Emerson College
128 Beacon Street
Boston 16, Massachusetts

Art Institute of Chicago
Goodman Memorial Theater
Chicago 3, Illinois

The '92 Theater
Wesleyan College
Middletown, Connecticut

Yale University School of   (Great, of course.)
    Drama
New Haven, Connecticut

Le Petit Théâtre du Vieux
    Carré
St. Peter's Street
New Orleans, Louisiana

The Carolina Playmakers   (Thomas Wolfe went here.)
University of North Carolina
Chapel Hill, North Carolina

So there. If you want to go on the stage, or into movies
or television, write to some of those people. They can
help you.

A word about television. Miss Burch, who casts those nine thousand actors a year, tells me that the ratio is ten men to every woman; this may be because of the enormous trend toward Westerns, which are hard on men and horses. TV prefers experienced actors, takes on very few newcomers, is harder to crack than movies. Girls sometimes break into pictures on the strength, merely, of an off-beat personality or a fancy figure. But TV is more demanding. With fewer pictures being made every year you'd better take pains to be a trained performer.

Ruth Burch adds this: "In advising young people who want to try their luck in television, motion pictures, or on Broadway, I cannot overemphasize one point: ambition alone is not enough. Don't come to Hollywood or go to New York unless you have confidence in yourself plus a bankroll to tide you over at least six months. But first get as much experience as possible with a local group in your home town—at your radio or TV station, with a little theater group, in summer stock, or with a college or high school dramatic group."

My own life as an actress has been happy, but I'm not at all sure that professional acting, especially at the star level, is the happiest kind of life for women.

You give up any idea of a private life the moment your name goes up in lights. Hollywood gossip is cruel and cynical. Hollywood is not the Heaven on Earth that the dime store girls and the Park Avenue girls seem to think it is—it is a competitive factory town.

Movie people, all of them, have what Gilbert Seldes calls "a high potential capacity for disaster." Home life, family life, marriage, is impaired by celebrity. Money begins to take on a strange value. And the temptations are real.

"Actors and actresses are handsome people and they work with many other handsome people; if Hollywood were run by a Puritan Gestapo, temptation would still thrive," says Leo C. Rosten. "As long as the making of films requires beautiful women and arresting men, especially men and women who can turn emotion on and off at the click of a camera shutter, Hollywood's amorous sentiments will be characterized by flexibility. . . . The making of films is a kind of prolonged fantasy, and picture-makers must be rich in reverie and capable of externalizing their inner foibles. Such people are not distinguished for emotional consistency."

We are not, it seems to me, as inconsistent as all that. The divorce rate in Hollywood is not higher than it is in Chicago, or New York, or Detroit. It just gets more publicity. Nevertheless, I have listed fourteen long-time happily married Hollywood couples—and I am superstitiously afraid to name them here. I'm told that every time you brag about a happy Hollywood marriage it breaks up before you can get into print.

If you want to come to Hollywood, think it over carefully. First, are you strong enough, do you know your craft, and are you really that ambitious? And would you like it for the rest of your life?

I like it. I would do everything all over again. But I can't help you, Marilyn and Janet, except in this hope: When you get to be a star, I'll gladly play a character part in your pictures.

Chapter 7

LET'S FACE IT

According to barrie, charm is "a sort of bloom on a woman. If you have it, you don't need to have anything else; and if you don't have it, it doesn't much matter what else you have."

Maggie Wylie says this in *What Every Woman Knows*. I don't recall how Maude Adams read the line, but no one who saw Helen Hayes at the Bijou in 1926 can ever forget how she bloomed with charm when she said it. And Maggie was supposed to be "plain."

You don't have to be a Tournament of Roses princess, or be as young as one, or try to look like one, to be charming. If you're past a certain age you'll only make a cartoon of yourself if you insist that youth can be re-created with mascara.

I saw myself in two motion pictures recently. One was made thirty years ago, with Robert Taylor and Greer Garson, and I looked so much younger (possibly thirty years younger) than I do now that I began to feel like an old onion. Then Warner Bros. previewed a new picture in which I play a mature woman with good sense and a good deal of money—"a character part," my daughter observed—and I liked myself even better. I would have looked idiotic and would have felt idiotic if I'd gone on as a soubrette.

Many a woman has lost out because she insisted on playing the ingénue when she should have played the mother, often the more rewarding part. This applies on Main Street and Park Avenue as well as in Hollywood.

A woman past forty should make up her mind to be young, not her face. I mean to say, don't try to make your face the way it was long years ago or you'll only succeed in destroying your own particular charm—the charm of experience, love, understanding, tolerance, sense of humor, even suffering, which molds and drama-tizes character. Why cover this up and look like a painted egg?

I am going to dig into my make-up kit in a moment, with the aid of Max Factor, Jr., and tell some professional secrets for the older woman. We need help, much more careful help than the pink beauty of twenty who can do absurd things to her hair or slap on color like a color-blind Picasso, and still look amusing, if absurd—sometimes amusing because she *is* absurd.

So I have some specific things to say as an actress about faces that are no longer twenty and shouldn't look like trying-to-be-twenty.

On stage or on screen I use a great deal of make-up, as any performer does, including men and the youngest girls, because of the fierce lights which tend to wash you out. But off stage what you see is mostly me with a minimum of retouching. Unless I'm wearing the white gloves I'm fond of you can have a good look at the freckles on my arms. I used to be ashamed of the freckles when I was very young. Now I point out that they look healthy, and besides, they are a good conversation piece.

"Why yes," it's fun to say, "I have been outdoors once or twice. Did you think I came off a whatnot?"

Women in their mature years should be more beautiful than they ever were in their twenties, thirties and forties. Max Factor, Jr., with whom I often consult, agrees with me. A woman with years of personal grooming practice should have learned to be nearly as skillful as a professional. And maturer women are supposed to be smart enough not to cling to outmoded make-up colors and techniques which they have outgrown.

Let's start basically. Never use a foundation make-up which is several shades lighter or darker than your own skin. Darker shades accentuate lines and hollows and lighter shades are too obviously a cover-up. A matching, harmonizing shade of foundation make-up will lop off years for you, without that absurd reaching-for-youth-which-ain't-there look.

Just because you're getting older—as who isn't?—don't let some misguided friend prevent you from using eye make-up. But don't fringe your eyes raggedy black to look like burnt holes in a shawl. Your eyes need definition, but this must be soft and carefully applied. Black eyebrow pencil and eyelash make-up are harsh. They pick up shadows. Instead, choose brown shades and apply them with feather-light touches. This is true even if your hair is black; soften the look with brown, or mix brown with the black. Be sure to pat face powder over your eyelids so they will look young and smooth. Have a care there, girl; don't put on so much that you blink up a cloud of powder when you bat your eyes.

Even if your eyes are not blue have a look at yourself with a hint of blue eye shadow—not for your eyes, but because this will add sparkle to your hair. This is especially true if you have silvery hair. Accent your eyes (gently does it!) for a new little personal drama.

At any rate, don't be afraid, be a little adventurous with your eyes. That's what they're for. Eyebrow and eye outlines that are indefinite, pale, and scattered leave only the iris or the pupil of the eye as the focal point with only the weak help of little lines and wrinkles for expression. Keep in mind that young brows are always defined and arched. Use a sharp eyebrow pencil, pluck away all stray hairs that confuse and blur the arch. Be feathery soft for daylight, more dramatic at night.

If your brows have turned gray or are entirely white, tint them with a brown pencil. Then take a clean, dry eyebrow brush, pass it over the pencil's "lead" until it is filled with color, and lightly brush the color in. Taper the arch out toward the temples. *After your hair has turned white or gray, never use a black pencil.*

Mascara? Be wary. Black is hard-looking, artificial, clownish, even for many very young women. Older women should stay with the rich warm brown tones, and with a very dry brush. Do you want to look as if you had tar on your eyes?

Don't put on a lot and then try to take it off. Use a little, then add a little. There is nothing more appalling than an elderly girl with gooy black eyelids and an orange-red mouth that looks like a saber wound.

I myself use very little powder but I use some. Scrubbing with rough washcloths is the best facial treatment I know of—that and rose water and glycerine.

Here is the Billie Burke unpatented formula for that:

> Glycerine 25%
> Natural oil of rose 0.1%
> Bay Rum (imported) 50%
> Tincture of benzoin 0.1%
> Distilled water for the remainder

This will keep your face and neck fresh, smooth and natural but not oily. I have my glycerine and rose water made up at Allen's Pharmacy, 9730 Wilshire Boulevard, Los Angeles. It costs $2.50 a pint.

And scrub. At the risk of being accused of being subsidized by the washcloth industry, I say again and again and again—wash your face! Wash it with pure, delicate soap, and towel it. Stimulate it. The "scrubbed look," which characterizes the American girl today, isn't patented by her. You too can become a scrublady.

In addition to this I stand on my head. I have been doing this for years, every morning, so it comes easy and is not dangerous for me now. If you can do it, there is nothing save the washcloth that will give you a better tone, a feeling of well-being, and a complexion. But pray don't attempt this unless you're balanced against the wall and sure you can get down without breaking a leg. The publishers and I take no responsibility for grandmas who stand on their heads without knowing how.

Back to powder. The matte finish is what we want here, the petal texture look. Avoid a sheen, which looks hard and which highlights the bone structure of your face. The matte finish absorbs light and a smooth, more youthful surface is what you get. Don't add layers of powder, especially if you have some wrinkles. You'll look an epoch or so older that way, with chalky lines creasing your face.

But the wrinkles are there, are they, and what to do about them? One thing is avoid getting any more by worrying about them. But begin at once to take care of your skin. If it has become dry, or dry in patches around your eyes, mouth, and neck, you are showing age beyond your years. You don't have to. Use daily creams containing moisturizers, foundation make-up containing moisturizers, and use cleansing creams that stimulate your skin.

But like all actresses, or all women, I have my favorite

beauty preparations. I highly recommend French cosmetics by Stendhal. I use their fresheners, cleansers, their day and night creams, and their face powder.

It's odd, but I suspect that many women who stare at themselves a great deal in mirrors do so only to admire their best "sides." They forget to take a good look at their necks, which may not be as flawless as they think. If you discover that your skin is getting leathery or spotty, it's possible that you can do something about it quickly.

Concentrate on the sides of your neck after your evening bath. Massage it with cream in a circular motion until your skin tingles. Pin your hair behind your ears, pat off the excess oils with tissue. When you use astringent or freshener on your face, don't forget your neck.

Along with the old girl who drips mascara, which makes her look more like a hag than a honey, I think the old girl who tints her hair pink or blue is a horror. Tinted hair is neither smart nor distinguished, except for retired madams in flappy dressing gowns raising rabbits in the Valley.

More than that, tinted hair has precisely the opposite effect from what you want. Its flamboyance and harshness makes a young face look older and an old face look older still.

If your hair is gray or white, keep it that way. Some women whose white hair turns yellow around their faces actually believe this makes them look blond and young. It doesn't. It merely frames their faces with soiled hair.

Keep white hair snow-white for the flattering highlights it will produce. Gray hair isn't really gray, you know. There is no such thing. Gray hair is merely a mixture of dark and white hair.

But you can blend this with a careful rinse and enjoy an all-over, steel-gray color. Women with blue, gray, or violet eyes find this kind of tint as flattering as a mink coat. But don't, for heaven's sake, go blue or mauve.

And never style your hair, if it is gray or white, so that strands show on the side of your face. When studio make-up men want to create witches their standard trick is to let hair hang in strings around the face. No matter how girlish you think you look in front of your private mirror, tuck it in when you go out. Do your hair up and away from your face. Watch what the actresses do. The upswept coiffure lifts sagging lines in the face, a scenic effect well-known in the theater.

And make it shine. Coax highlights into your hair. Keep the gleams alight with shampoos. Emphasize big, deep waves which sparkle and dip and swirl. Never have your gray or white hair done in tight, small waves and curls. Don't slick it back in a boyish bob, and don't pull it tight, with a severe bun, like a Spanish ballroom dancer, unless you are a Spanish ballroom dancer.

Never use orange rouge or lipstick, or deep raspberry

shades. Orange tends to yellow gray or white hair and the raspberry is overdramatic, painted-looking. Instead, use pastel rouges and harmonizing clear lipstick reds, roses, and pinks.

Another don't: Never spray white or gray hair with perfume. There are ladies who seem to think this is a sophisticated touch of special elegance, but it isn't. The perfume will turn your hair yellow, precisely what you want to avoid. Never go further with perfume than a little spot behind the ear lobe. And don't hide all your hair with a hat or allow only a tuft to show. Choose your hat according to the shape of your face (and the shape of your pocketbook) but let it be a modification of the current fashion, not the whole striking fashion, when that fashion is not for you.

Above all, to repeat and repeat and repeat, *do not change the natural color of your hair*. Gray hair comes along providentially, just when we need it to soften our faces. Let it alone and take full advantage of it.

But don't avoid all color in your clothes, which are part of your make-up. Beiges, silver, and warm grays, blues, dusty pinks, roses, soft greens, corals, heather mixtures light in tone, and almost any pastels—those are the ones to use. Stay away from black unless you use it smartly. Bright-skinned youth can wear black, but older women who put it on, following a fashion, often turn out looking funereal. Exception: You can wear black if you light up your face with a white or pastel scarf, or if you wear a black hat as a dramatic frame for white hair.

Some women turn to lavender, violet, or purple as proper colors for maturity. Some feel that these are their "special colors," and arrange entire ensembles in one, or all, of these shades. It's a mistake. Even the very young shouldn't wear them—there are no lavenders or purples in the skin except in shadows, or in places that shouldn't be there, as in blotches and bruises. If your skin is unusually bright and youthful-looking, of course you can wear anything.

Red nails? That depends on your skin. If your hands are white, really white, O.K. But certainly not red if your hands are brown, as most older hands are, or your knuckles are enlarged. Why call attention? Instead, just keep your nails neat and clean. As for toenails, I'd suggest that you keep them in your shoes with your feet where they belong.

Sum it all up and we're back to Barrie and his blooming charm. Which, I think, means "Be yourself." Which reminds me:

More years than I'm going to tell you ago, in London, I begged for the part of Peter Pan and didn't get it. Dion Boucicault gave it to Pauline Chase, who had better legs. Then came Maude Adams, who made the part so thoroughly her own for so many years that I can't recall any other actress intrepid enough to play it until a brave—and gorgeous—and very young actress named Betty Bronson, who was chosen by Barrie himself, made the movie in 1925.

I saw Betty the other day. She retired from the screen some years ago, at the height of her young beauty. She is the wife of Ludwig Lauerhass, vice-president of the Stuart Co., in Pasadena, a civic worker, an occasional newspaper columnist, a sculptor (talented, but she studied and worked hard to learn how), a magnificent cook, a mother-in-law, and a grandmother.

"Peter Pan," of all people, a grandmother!

But handsomer, smarter-looking than ever before with a gay scarf at her throat, a mere trace of light lipstick, and soft, wavy, burnished gray hair.

She's vital, interested in other people—and unre-touched. She photographs so beautifully (the gray hair is the key there) that I'm sure she could get all the movie roles she wanted if she wanted 'em.

Betty, with all the professional skill a great movie star is bound to have, doesn't do a thing to herself you can't do too. Isn't that what Barrie had in mind?

Chapter 8

HOW TO STEAL UP TO TEN DOLLARS AND OTHER GOOD ADVICE

MEN LIKE to complain about women. Grousing about the follies and shortcomings of females is fun for the male and is part of a masculine ritual which says, "See here, little girl, I am a great, wise chief while you are a small, foolish, and helpless creature who depends on my prowess and know-how for happiness and survival."

This isn't so, as every woman knows at least by the time she is eight years old, but this is what a husband is saying and feeling good about when he brays in the bathroom over a tube of toothpaste squeezed in the middle.

Any all-American husband can enjoy a full evening of despair over a smidge of misshaped Ipana. This makes him feel fine and does you no harm; he expects you to be efficient with a skillet, perhaps, but in many other areas he dotes on a number of standard foibles. He associates them with femaleness.

The trick is to know when you are driving a man beyond the bragging point—to know whether you have stirred him too far or whether he is merely reacting to a cartoon about wives in *The Saturday Evening Post*. As every woman who lives with a man always learns, men enjoy grumbling about women because it makes them feel so superior. This is all right, too. By inference this makes a woman more feminine and desirable.

A standard complaint is the chaos of a woman's pocketbook. Art Linkletter, a shrewd fellow, uses this cliché on his coast-to-coast television show and everybody likes it. He would be dismayed, and some husband would conclude that he'd inadvertently married a mechanical monster, if a wife's purse once showed up in apple-pie order, like the FBI files.

Men complain that "feminine logic" is outrageous—knowing better but feeling better every time they say it. No husband worth having will let you call his wife a fool, but he will call her one in many complimentary ways.

They mumble about the length of wife-to-wife telephone conversations as if the wives were pre-empting the Atlantic cable while Ike and Macmillan were waiting to get in a word edgeways. But they expect their girls to talk their heads off and yak themselves happy. It's what gals do and they wouldn't have it if their girls were "different."

They pretend dismay, sometimes with enormous conviction, about wives' entries in checkbook stubs. One gentleman I know says that his wife "writes with her hair when she keeps books." He made up that phrase and repeats it at every opportunity, with pride. As a matter of fact, mathematics and economics beyond the fifth-grade level baffle him, although he has talent. He would be dismayed and affronted if his wife handled figures like a Certified Public Accountant. (This one probably could, but she enjoys the joke, too.)

Husbands roar in horror or make piteous noises about extravagance. This is purely a feminine word. It does not equate with "investment," as in the purchase of fishing tackle, golf balls, or a 22-foot yawl, which a man requires to entertain accounts or to keep up his strength to support her.

Unless a wife is really behaving like a fiscal idiot (I know that some do, and they should be put on stern allowances), most men are bragging when they thunder to their friends about how their wives think money grows on trees to be thrown to birds. In my experience, which is pretty long, I've known many husbands who made out that their wives were buying department stores when, actually, the wives were practicing the most cunning economies—and the husbands were very proud of it. The complainer was merely beating his chest. He was announcing to other men that he had captured a very desirable woman who required a lot of upkeep—and he, of course, was the little old boy who could keep her, too.

These husbandly wails—and I could make this list much longer—are part of a long, lugubrious, standard list. A wise wife plays up to them and keeps her man feeling able and in good voice.

Then we come to an innocuous-seeming file which has to be taken seriously. These, too, are hackneyed—but please note this difference: Men never brag about them.

Have you wondered, sometimes, why your husband, who's the best storyteller and yarn-maker-upper in your crowd, suddenly turned sullen at a party, or spent the evening in a corner with a model (and he thinks models are morons), and wouldn't talk all the way home?

It could be that you innocently interrupted him, pointing out that he saw that three-toed bear on a vacation in June, not July, because in July Alfred had his tonsils out, and that was the time you didn't have a maid, either.

Let the man finish his story, woman. Even if he gets it wrong. Even if he's lying. Especially if he's lying. The man doesn't live, dear, who doesn't consider himself the most fascinating raconteur in the world, and he doesn't want prompting from the wings.

Incidentally, the often-printed advice which says you must listen to your husband's old stories with fresh and eager interest even if you've heard them a hundred and a half times is a bromide and an untruth. *Don't* listen. He'd much rather you didn't. You'll either look bored or you'll threaten him with corrections.

I have interviewed some husbands about what wives do that really annoys them. My son-in-law tactfully said that his wife, my daughter, never under any circumstances offended him in any way. Never.

Then, as he patiently turned purple, he said that it did occur to him, for God's sake, that he wished that woman would either leave dresser drawers all the way open or all the way closed instead of just a *little* open. It seems to him, he said, that he goes around all day closing dresser drawers that are a *little* open.

Another young husband, who obviously thinks his wife is the most delicious bit of fluff that ever came along, also swore that his girl was unquestionably perfect. He does not criticize her at all for playing bridge so late every afternoon that dinner is usually a hasty apology. He knows she spends too much for clothes but he likes to see her look smart. But he is offended and puzzled by wads of used Kleenex which dot the house, from bedroom to breakfast room.

I don't know why it is that even impeccable girls, the scrubbed-look kind, who are quick to scold a husband if he tracks mud or spills a little ash, are sometimes themselves "a little careless around the edges." But all of us are careless and we have to watch it. Men have those big muscles, or ought to have them, but they are curiously sensitive creatures about many small things. Often, if a woman can learn to avoid that one small thing which makes a gent palpitate and wince, she can train him to put up with almost everything else.

Another standard complaint is that men who live with women have no property rights.

Wives, daughters, mothers-in-law, cousins, and aunts, if they are afforded room and board under a man's roof, assume as a matter of course that all personal male property is theirs by right of conquest. Nothing in masculine ownership is sacred, including even the treasures of small boys, who are often very bitter about the disappearance of knives, balls of twine, and collections of useful mechanical marvels from junk heaps. My grandson is in constant pain because "people keep stealing my stuff." The people always turn out to be females; his father scrupulously avoids "borrowing" so much as a tenpenny nail. This is part of a chivalric code which I guess women are just incapable of grasping.

At any rate, any man surrounded by women is re-signed to the eventual loss of his Eversharp, his pen, pocketknife, his keys to the car, his stamps, and his shirts, which teen-age daughters find attractive. He also knows that women do not consider it stealing to pinch money up to a ten-dollar bill.

I've been asking around about this ten-dollar-bill phobia and I can't get it explained. All I am sure of is that you can lift all the money you want so long as you don't filch a ten-spot. Men hold them in awe and even make a great to-do about getting them changed. Let ten-dollar bills alone, sister.

But men put up with feminine pilfering with no more than routine complaint. They beller but they don't take overt action. They call attention to their own high moral values, but they expect all women to steal. However, there is one cardinal sin. Let young wives pay attention:

Never, dear, positively never, borrow a man's screw driver and leave it out in the rain.

It may be a fine Sears and Roebuck tool or it may be a cheap dime-store instrument. It doesn't matter. It is a symbol, it *represents* something to a husband, it is *his*, his one and only piece of untouchable property. He may not use it. He may not know how to use it. You may need it and you may know how to use it, so go ahead (there's no use telling you not to), but *put it back*. And wipe it off if you used it to dig in the dahlia bed.

You can make all the errors in the list I have just finished and make them repeatedly and still keep your man, even if you don't keep him as happy as he'd like to be. Just be wary and try to avoid them. Commit them all regularly and you'll hear more bass noise around the house than is proper for your refined neighborhood.

The fundamental, hurtful mistakes that women make with men are usually found in situations we can all recognize, nearby, perhaps next door:

1. The wife who lacks faith in her husband's ability *and shows it*. He may need and want help, nudging, and inspiration, but if you, his wife, question his fundamental ability, you have emasculated him and you have killed him as a man.

Have faith. Faith begets confidence. Even if the faith is misplaced, it inspires something far more precious than success, or money, or position. It inspires love. Oh, I know a man who is just a little stupid. He can hold only the smallest position. He earns the meagerest salary. But he and his family are the happiest people I know—because his wife looks on him as a man, and she's in love with his manhood, and shows it, to him and to everybody, with every smile and glance.

2. The wife who constantly compares her husband with her father. It seems to me that this is a fairly widespread mistake. I could tell of one sad instance in which

a charming and ambitious young woman constantly held up the example of her rich and successful parent to an amiable and brilliant husband whose only fault was that he didn't resemble her father. The result was as bad as possible—a scandal and a broken marriage which could have been a happy marriage. As it turned out, the wife with the father fixation actually hated her father. She had married her husband, whom she deeply loved, *because* he was different from her father.

3. The wife who looks elsewhere for security than to her own husband. It doesn't matter where she looks, to her own ability, to her father, to her mother, or to her rich uncle. Many a weak man has been propped up and given potency because a wife was wise and patient, and enough of an actress, to create an illusion for him. Making a man of a man is sometimes a woman's chief job on earth. It's worth trying and the rewards are so very rich.

4. The wife who, with what I have just said lovingly in mind, makes the fatal error of insisting on changing her husband's career to suit her taste, her ambition, or her ideas of social status. A young woman in Burbank recently did just that. Her husband was happy, successful enough, and a charming man with a job as an accountant. Accountancy wasn't enough for our girl, who insisted that her husband should strike out on his own in a more glamorous field.

I must say he tried. He tried desperately hard. But his

new work embarrassed and terrified him. He sought escape in alcohol with the usual results. (I am a teetotaler, I would be a Prohibitionist if I thought Prohibition would work; I am against drinking. But to be accurate, we have to admit that alcohol is not always the cause of all failures. Alcohol itself is sometimes an escape from something else.)

5. The wife who takes advantage of the situation—the situation being that the man is in love with her—and contrives to avoid her responsible share of the work of running a home and a marriage. This gal, who depends upon her husband to do the shopping, take the children to school, and help the kids with their homework, meantime making enough money to keep her as a pet—well, she exists and she is a fool, but fortunately she is a rare article. Today's young wife is a proud and finely tempered woman who does her share and more. Just don't slip when you discover that a good man is willing to work himself to death for you. He may do exactly that.

6. The wife who is jealous of her husband because her chores as a housewife, cleaning woman, and baby tender are dull and hard while his job in an air-conditioned office, with two hours for lunch and an expense account, seems easy and exciting. I believe that this feminine jealousy of the male is far more widespread than is generally realized, and for a good reason: Housework is dull, especially for a bright and educated girl, and eight

hours a day in the glass-plated, chromium corporation world of business *is* more exciting. But be thoughtful before you whine that it's a man's world. It's also a competitive, ruthless, and killing world. If your man is going to get ahead in it he needs you and the security and the reason for trying that you give him. Keep in mind that his bosses know all about you; a junior executive these days doesn't get promoted far, if at all, unless the Big Brass knows it can safely promote his wife along with him. In the long run, and it is a long run, any marriage is, your job may be not only as important as his but easier and certainly less lethal.

Sometimes, as I grab for my notes and say things, I seem to be saying them too starkly. I seem to be saying: "Do this, or don't do this, and wham! There goes your marriage!"

No such thing, of course. I'm not that wise. But it does seem to me that wives have a major job which, sometimes, they refuse to consider as a job at all. Marriage, a young girl thinks, is a continuous romance, a lark, a romp. Well, it's no such thing, my dear young person. And men are more sensitive than you thought and often very hard people to live with.

Yes, heavens knows, husbands are faulty animals at best. They are in rather a bad way at the moment, as all the psychologists and magazine writers have been pointing out. They have lost dignity as fathers and as heads-of-family. Paradoxically, just as they are making more money than ever before, they have lost their places of honor. The average American home today, it seems to me, is commanded by teen-agers, not by the authoritarian father of a few decades ago.

If husband-father is going to be put back somewhere near his proper place, which is where every wife wants him for her own security and happiness, then we women have got to prepare that place. After all, as I keep saying, we set the stage.

Chapter 9

CLOTHES—AND THE SHAPE YOU'RE IN

As I said before, I always thought that the chief reason for the success I had on the Broadway stage as a young woman was my clothes. They were new and high-style for their time, fresh, immaculate—and expensive. Most of them were designed and made in Paris.

Over the years, I learned a few things about fashion and I pay the most particular attention to fashion now— but oh my, not nearly so expensively as I used to! The most important thing I learned was to get the best advice I could from the best experts.

That is why I am not writing this chapter about

clothes for the maturing woman. I have called in an expert, and I present her with pride.

You know her as the famous "Renie" of Hollywood. Renie designed all the costumes for Disneyland. For the past five years she has designed the costumes, indeed the whole production, of Shipstead and Johnston's Ice Follies. *She has designed clothes for all the major stars in Hollywood for the past fifteen years, for Garbo, Norma Shearer, Joan Crawford, Ginger Rogers, Irene Dunne, Joan Fontaine—and for Clark Gable.*

Renie is an expert at the rumba and the samba, and holds three trophies as an amateur speed skater on ice. Her full name is Mrs. Leland Hawes Conley and she is a grandmother.

Are you, or are you about to be a grandmother? Then pay attention to Renie.

At any age in life, including the cradle if the baby is a girl, *color* and *line* are the governing factors that make the difference between being smartly and correctly dressed and being dowdy. Color and line control our choices whether we know it or not. As we grow more mature, past the careless years when we could get away with anything from a sack to tight breeches, or sunburn and the wrong lipstick, we have to be increasingly aware of what we put on ourselves and whether it matches us.

Our coloring changes as we grow older. This is as

certain as the difference between the pastel buds of spring and the full-flowered blossoms of summer—and what are we going to do about it?

The best attitude is an adventurous point of view. Let's consider our changing looks as a challenging experience but not—as too many ill-advised and worried women do—as an inspiration to dye our hair willy-nilly, on the advice of an overeager bridge partner, in a foolish attempt to hang onto our foolish youth. And even worse, let's not go into a panic, or a sulk, and "just give the whole thing up."

There are definite, intelligent things to do and we'll take them up right now, one by one.

Color

Perhaps you have always worn strong, bright colors. Suddenly they don't look right next to your face—the eyes seem to "disappear" and the hair looks washed out. Or you have always loved grays and beiges—and now, you think, they make you look all one color—not the chic "one-color" look sometimes advocated by the fashion magazines, but a washed-in-one look that is drab and discouraging. What is to be done about that?

First, you must decide that you are going to be interested in a whole new color range for your personal clothes. After you have accepted this, and the idea that

perhaps you are going to look more interesting than you
have ever looked before, start with your hair and make-
up. If possible, go to an expert. (Former remarks about
hair dyeing refer to the hard, obvious kind that a lot of
women achieve with a bottle and an old toothbrush.)
Even one visit with a smart technician will give you a
new interest in yourself. You will enjoy at least the faint
hope that all is not lost, that it is truly possible to be attractive in your own way, at any rate more pleasant-
looking. The proper kind of rinse will put life back into
your hair, and wonderful things can be done with make-
up. From an expert you can learn the art yourself, if
there's not time or money for a regular program. One of
the professional tricks you will learn is to use make-up
sparingly but strategically. An example is new "color"
and "line" for your eyebrows, and a new, younger expression.

Now that you have a "new face," start trying some
different colors in clothes. Black can be trying, perhaps,
but be sure. Don't accept over-all statements about what
to do after forty. Reaction to colors is as individual as
fingerprints. Navy blue with a very deep brown is a surprise combination that I came across in Paris once, where
I saw the famous milliner Paulette actually transform a
woman's face with these colors. A very deep, rich brown
can sometimes be a pleasant surprise. (On a recent picture, I persuaded Clark Gable to wear a brown costume

instead of a black one. In his color tests he looked ten years younger.)

Be very careful of gray. Be sure it does not wash out the warm tints of your skin—but try it. Some warm grays, with a touch of soft color next to the face, can be enchanting with gray hair.

Don't choose a cold gray tone. The best thing is to get some scarves or pieces of fabric, sit down in front of a mirror in a good light, and look at yourself as you try the various colors under your chin and next to your face. Which ones make your eyes look darker and bigger? Which give your hair more interest?

If you love bright colors, try a simple basic color for your dress and then add bits of your favorite shade with a scarf or a string of beads. The "safe" course is always a basic color with pearls under your chin. There is something about the sheen of pearls that does more for the feminine face than almost anything else. Have you noticed that through the years the Duchess of Windsor has almost always worn a string of pearls? Look up some photographs of her in old fashion magazines and see for yourself. She usually complements the pearls with fresh white gloves.

But sometimes an older woman needs the flamboyance of bright color. If it makes you happy, try it. If you have to cope with a timid husband then experiment at home before making a splash at the country club. Even a shocking-pink nightgown might do fine things for your view on life, and his—what's the harm? Or a bright blue slip may make an older woman feel that life still holds many more gay moments. Why not be bold enough to try a few colorful indulgences? It's a very harmless way of being adventurous.

Don't at any age hide in the dreadful anonymity of the small print dress, all too often in an inexpensive "practical" color. Nothing is more unattractive, more truly lacking in interest and distinction, and all too often it becomes a uniform. There is no excuse for arguing that it is the type of dress that "wears well." Better, at all times, a solid color in a pleasant shade than this granny garment which is always found in the "older woman's" section.

Line

Now we come to what most women call "style." Style is just changing line. And "line" means just that—the line clothes make on your body. Will you become a triangle, or a balloon, or a small square top, protruding below, or a wedge?

These are general style terms covering the general silhouette of any period in fashion. Every change brings some new and fancy terminology to designate line. *The style of the dress is the line it makes on your body*, or of your body. The line may be good or bad for you.

Generally, women get heavier or lose weight as they grow older—sad to say, the twenty-year-old figure is almost the exclusive copyright of the twenty-year-olds; a woman past forty is rather ill-advised to try to dress like one or act like one unless her name is Dietrich.

If you have grown heavier, your chief problem is that the shops do not stock pretty dresses for the mature figure. You have to hunt for those that are attractive, make your own, or have them made. But it is ridiculous to think that you can't look smart and pretty, even if you have a weight problem that seemingly won't melt away.

Plan a pretty neckline, a flattering one for you, as your first step in selecting a dress. Do what motion picture stars and their designers do—concentrate on the neckline, the face-framing, important part of your costume. Billie Burke has always excelled at this. Fluffy, soft bows —"kitten-ear bows," designers call them—have been a part of her costumes for years; soft, draped collars are another touch of hers that add an illusion of softness to a more mature face—and in my opinion *any* face needs some flattery.

If your neck is not as attractive as you could wish and you haven't the time or the energy to correct it, then cover it with soft chiffon scarves or pretty collars turned up high. The velvet neckband of the dowager type is gone forever, we hope, but the idea remains for us to use in our own way today. Almost everyone needs a soft collar of some type—this is why shirtwaist dresses go on forever. They are always flattering. If you wear a plain type of neckline, dress it up with pearls or some such device for a softer look.

As a rule, the mature figure looks better in a blouse or "top" that is not strictly fitted. A bit of ease and soft blousing without losing the basic lines of a dress is pleasanter and more comfortable and more beguiling. Avoid the "sausage" look. Only movie stars and the very young should wear tight sweaters, fitted bosoms, and the rest of that decidedly un-chic nonsense.

Skirts can be interesting even though you have a fifty hip—they truly can. They can't grab you too tightly, can't be full of pleats, but they can be carefully cut and fitted to fall in graceful bias folds which fit softly at the hip and move with ease and grace when you walk. I have made them for actresses who had to walk in front of the camera hundreds of times during the filming of a picture, and this is the hardest test of all for the necessary feeling of ease in wearing a garment.

If you have grown thinner, and in places where you wish you hadn't, you can still be chic and outstanding. Again, by *line* you can make the body appear rounder and more feminine. The advantage of the thin figure is that the waist is usually small. Depending upon the amount you wish to pay, you can be dressed by Balenciaga or by Sears, but you have a wide choice. Your problem is selection. Many styles are young and lacking in dignity or distinction for the mature woman, so when in doubt, strive to be elegant. This is most often achieved by being conservative.

Body

We've been discussing the basics of clothing, line and color, for any year or age. Now a word about the shape you're in.

We're lucky today. With all the easily available gyms, swimming pools, and various kinds of beauty and reducing studios and home devices, even a water-whirley to soothe off the pounds as you bathe, you may be as passive or as vigorous as you wish and still improve your figure. Tests have been made for a long time which show that exercise can be continued for an indefinite period, up to almost any age. Ruth St. Denis, who is certainly a mature woman (mature enough to put her age in *Who's Who*; it's seventy-nine) still uses her body beautifully and accomplishes lovely, fluid movements with it in dance recitals. Martha Graham is another woman past fifty whose body is in magnificent condition. She has just completed an exciting and successful trip to the Orient with her dance company. So, unless there is a specific health reason for it, the modern woman has the means to keep her figure trim and elastic regardless of years. The better the figure, the better-looking the clothes you put on it.

Even with the worst figure possible there are still things to do for improvement. Posture, sitting and standing, are first and foremost. It pays to concentrate on them. The most beautiful dress in the world can be ruined by a slouch or a sprawl. Each epoch and age has had its notion of attractive posture. In the early twelfth and thirteenth centuries, all women of fashion tried to look pregnant. Skirts were draped so as to give an illusion of fullness at front and many medieval statues of women of this period are shown with hands tucked under the front draperies to give their stomachs a fuller look. If you remember the motion picture *Henry V*, you will remember this look. Then there was the Irene Castle period. All of you recall pictures of her—body swayed forward, one leg reaching back, toe pointing, head high? A lovely, floating look. Then we had the flapper era with pelvis pressed well forward, the upper body concave so that the bosom was flattened, head protruding, and over-all a lean, lank, boyish look.

Current Fashion Posture

We are now in a period of the stand-up-straight-and-look-elegant. Audrey Hepburn is an outstanding example of this wonderful, regal type of carriage. Based, of course, on ballet, it frees the body to move with grace in any direction—looks the world in the face and moves forth to conquer.

Are you following this ideal? Or do you slouch in your chair, sit with legs spread in a widened arc (a horrid habit of mature women) or walk with limp shoulders as though you were carrying a heavy bucket in each hand? Results of this: a lump at the back of the neck and slack muscles. You lumber instead of walk. The entire posture is unattractive.

Don't just sigh and say, "Well, I'm getting older." More nearly the truth would be, "I'm getting lazier." All of us can stand straight, walk with heads erect, and look and move with a certain amount of grace. Try this little test: Pick out a very attractive woman who is sitting down—at a party or restaurant, and watch what happens when she gets up. Most of the time the illusion of attractiveness vanishes as she scrambles to her feet and moves away bunched over, with uncertain, hurried movements. Poise, along with leisurely, sure movements are more and more necessary as we grow older.

In this department, every woman can improve herself without spending a dime for professional help. Watch graceless women move, stand, get up, and walk as if they creaked with effort, then make it look effortless when you do it. Don't lean forward like a football player about to charge, then push yourself up with straining arms.

Plant your feet firmly and *get up*. It'll look good, be good, and feel good.

Shoes

Discussion of movements brings us to shoes. (Don't forget you can flounder or totter in flats as well as in higher-heeled footgear.) What hideousness is sold to women under the guise of comfort! What horrors of "wedgies," what dreadful "open-work" monstrosities with sensible heels! True, some women have abused their feet and have to wear a certain type of low-heeled shoe. Aching feet are a very unpleasant experience that eventually shows in the face. But nowadays there are attractive, well-styled shoes of great comfort and good looks, low- or medium-heeled. They are cut with line and style; hunt them out. Possibly they have been designed for a younger generation, but just because a clerk takes a look at your gray hair, don't let him bring you a "gray-haired shoe."

Lower heels are fine for walking, marketing, and other workaday chores, but why does one assume (just because the calendar says so many years have gone by) that pretty high-heeled shoes are out of the question? Treat yourself to several pairs, and treat your family and friends to the lovely look of a pretty foot. A higher heel gives a different look to the leg. It isn't just happenstance that "cheese-cake" photographs show their models in high heels. Photographers know that heels give a different stance, a different look to the leg. Right now, with shorter skirts the fashion, it is something to consider; and since many fashionable women of all ages never lower or raise their hemlines more than an inch or so (one of New York's best-dressed women has not changed her hemline more than that in fifteen years) it is something to keep in mind at all times.

I also believe that occasionally wearing flat "flats" will keep feet mobile and flexible. If they are not comfortable, wear them for only an hour or so. The Achilles tendon at the back of the heel tends to shorten with age, and this is a healthy way to stretch it.

Do shop carefully for shoes—be sure they fit, get larger sizes if necessary, and keep in mind simple, well-cut shoes. Even with a foot problem, these can still be found for comfortable wear.

Slacks and Sports Clothes

What about slacks, shorts, and bathing suits for the mature woman who would like to be a part of the current trend?

If she has kept her figure, she hasn't too many problems with this part of the wardrobe, but she has some. Even if she has stayed reasonably slender, she is likely to be plagued by that softened inner-thigh muscle, likely to sag below a short bathing suit. Cover it up! It is possible to buy wonderful bathing suits now with all sorts of built-in gadgets, and with longer flattering skirts that are more than kind to this leg muscle. If you have other leg difficulties, forget about them if you like to swim, and swim anyway. Just pick the prettiest, most attractive, soft kind of suit you can find in one-color pattern, get a short coat to cover you when you are sitting around on the beach—and have fun.

A tight lastex suit in brilliant color, or a too short suit, can be ridiculous on a less-than-perfect figure; but even a quite heavy figure can look smart and comfortable in the right suit, which looks "easy" and has been cut to conceal bulges. It is well worth the time it takes to find it. A pretty, large beach hat is a flattering accessory for the older woman, and it helps take care of the problem of too much sun on an older skin. Look as pretty as you can, don't be conspicuous, don't be self-conscious, and swim the rest of your life if you want to.

The older woman who wants to wear shorts at home or in her own patio for comfort should do so—but don't go to market or out on the street unless you happen to be the fortunate one in a thousand whose legs and figure are trim. Shorts seem to accentuate a stomach and heavy hips—not to mention what they do to too-heavy or too-thin legs. The older woman should not buy shorts that

Vasiliu

are too short in the leg, nor should she buy the Bermuda length unless she is long-legged. It's a matter of proportion, and the only way to find the correct length is to keep trying them on until the legline looks right. A full-length mirror is a good idea, and a rear-view mirror is essential. Most women would never wear shorts again if they got one good look at themselves in pants too tight or too baggy—and many wouldn't wear them if they got one good look at themselves.

Nor can slacks be worn with impunity, even if they do cover you up. In general, they, too, should be restricted to home unless you are able to maintain a really lithe, whistle-inspiring figure. And again the rear fit is most important. So is the proportion of fit in the legs. If you are heavy-hipped with medium-size legs, pants that are cut to mold the legs only succeed in exaggerating the hipline. On the other hand, if you are lucky enough to have a slim figure, and good legs, you should investigate the new "stretch" pants; they will do for your tummy and fanny very much the same good work as a stretch girdle, and they are a joy to wear.

Hats

Hats are great fun for the older woman. They are flattering, attention-getting, conversation pieces (look at Hedda Hopper), and generally a happy addition to a costume. But not the basic black straw, usually shiny with flowers, which appears in the spring, ditto the small shapeless white straw, also with flowers, which appears in the summer, and the dull felt which appears regularly each fall. Just look about you at any gathering of older women and you will see drab examples of what I mean.

A cheap hat can have style and line. A very expensive one can make you look ridiculous. If a hat doesn't make you look more attractive, don't buy it. This is what Billie Burke told me many years ago, when I designed her costumes for a film, and it is always and forever good advice. Just don't buy a hat unless it gives you a lift, makes your heart beat a bit faster, and makes you feel good. Even a hat from the hat bar can do all of these things. The kind to avoid are the "head-coverings," which are not one thing or another. If you choose the flower type, wear those hats with quite a few flowers—enough to look confident and opulent. One hat like this is worth the investment, and much better than several that are undistinguished.

Here again, it's all in the time you put in shopping. It is ridiculous to assume that because you haven't much money, you can't buy good things. Study the magazines, look in the windows of the good shops, and now and then go to a fashion show, even if some of the hats are imports that gave you a laugh when you saw pictures of them in print.

The ideal thing, of course, is to go to a really fine milliner and see what she selects for you. When Paulette, the famous Paris milliner, put one of her selections on my head for the first time, I was surprised and enchanted. The colors, the line, and the whole "look" were as unlike anything I had ever worn as could be imagined. But suddenly I saw how right the hat was and how much better a really fine milliner saw my face and head than I could see them. It is sometimes hard to be objective about yourself, but expert guidance brings rich rewards.

There are two courses open to a woman. Either she is bored or not interested in clothes, or she *is* interested. If not, then the sensible thing to do is not to fret about it. Go to someone and accept help, or evolve a basic type of dressing that makes you happy, and give the matter no further thought. Some women, curiously enough, who have followed this line of least resistance have emerged as great personalities in the rightness of what they always wear. It suits them—they are happy in forgetting what they have on, and that is a fine objective for them. Others would be miserable in this kind of arrangement. They need change and the stimulus of different types of clothes. They find excitement in studying the current fashion picture to find what's right for them, what fits into their particular lives.

Claudette Colbert once asked me if I ever wore long

evening dresses. I said I never did. My work and my family occupy me so much that I can't follow a social whirl that includes a lot of formal dress. Claudette said that she herself had bought a fabulous evening gown in Paris two years before because it was so beautiful, but she had never had it on. So you see even a movie star can go overboard on something just too much for any occasion.

I mention this because clothes should be selected for the kind of life one leads. Let's not buy a sidesaddle habit, even though it's fabulously becoming, unless we are riding to hounds.

A good objective, wardrobe-wise, is to be interesting, individual, and truly oneself, and still accord with the community in which one lives. What looks right in Hollywood doesn't always fit the scene in Connecticut— Hollywood might seem a bit too casual in certain Eastern scenes, and Connecticut country tweeds might not appear too necessary in the San Fernando Valley. But I think that you should always wear clothes that make you happy. With this, and good taste as an aim, you won't go too far wrong.

Please remember the basic things:

1. COLOR and LINE are the governing factors in everything you wear that shows.

2. As you grow a bit older, an entire new color

scheme can make you look more interesting than ever before.

3. LINE means the changing line of "style," and your best line is probably one that doesn't hug you too tight. To be elegant, be conservative.

4. A lot depends on the shape *you're* in. There is faint excuse these days for a sloppy figure.

5. Watch your posture! Learn how to get up gracefully from a table, never slouch, avoid that lump at the back of the neck. Make your movements leisurely and sure—and look years younger.

6. Good shoes are not necessarily the most expensive, and you do enjoy shopping, don't you? Seek them out. Remember what wonders high heels do for the feminine leg.

7. Before you purchase slacks, shorts, and other sports outfits, install a full-length mirror—with a rear view.

8. Hats are for fun.

9. Buy clothes that match you and conform to good style in your community—don't "go Hollywood" on Main Street, or Main Line in Las Vegas.

10. Best advice of all: Take a good look at yourself. Everybody else does!

Chapter 10

MY BEST ADVICE

I LIKE TO READ the "Best Advice" pieces in *Reader's Digest*. They are beautifully and clearly written and they are always wise. They baffle me, though, because they always make me try to think of the best advice I ever had, and I can't. I had so much advice. Everybody from Madame Louise Dauste de Fortis, my first dramatic teacher (who told me to go to Italy and study opera) to an audience in Birkenhead (which yelled at me, "Let's have it a little louder, duckie!") has advised me all my life about everything.

John Drew, Flo Ziegfeld, James M. Barrie, Booth

Tarkington and George Cukor have at one time or another given me fine advice—whatever it was. My milkman, my grocer, my grandson, Warner Bros. Studio, the William Morris Agency, and the Vice-President in charge of answering telephone calls from Billie Burke at Coward-McCann, Inc., publishers of this book, all give me sound advice. I am the kind of person that other people *do* advise.

Homer Croy, the handsome writer, recently gave me some first-rate advice. Homer said: "Don't listen to anybody, Billie. Do it your own way."

That's good advice, but I do listen. What happens after that, of course, is something else to consider.

I particularly liked what Helen Hayes said to her son James, now a very fine actor indeed, when he left New York for Hollywood to work in his first major television show. Helen said: "James, just try to achieve something and forget about success." (This appears in the *Digest* for September, 1958.)

I liked Sam Goldwyn's *Digest* advice: "... a man's most precious possession is his courage. No matter how black things seem, if you have courage, darkness can be overcome."

And the Rev. Dr. Harry Emerson Fosdick's quote from his father: "Tell Harry that he can cut the grass today, if he feels like it. Tell Harry he had better feel like it."

And Estes Kefauver's "Estes, you must turn your stumbling blocks into steppingstones. Let hurt feelings be a prod to work just that much harder."

How can anyone do better than accept these philosophies? Subscribe to *Reader's Digest*, $4 a year.

Marlon Brando has a motto in his living room that I think could be followed, too, with profit and rejoicing. It says: *You Aint Livin' If You Don't Know It.*

On a bulletin board in front of a Los Angeles church the other day I saw a sign that impressed me so much I remembered it. It said: *If You Want to Sing, You'll Find a Song.*

And consider these lines by David Herbert Lawrence: "One realm we have never conquered—the pure present. One great mystery of time is terra incognita to us—the instant. The most superb mystery we have hardly recognized, the immediate, instant self. The quick of all time is the instant."

To which we could add Walt Whitman's great "The whole theory of the Universe is directed unerringly to one single individual—namely, to YOU."

Those last paragraphs sum up, I believe, to what I was trying to say in another chapter: "Appreciate the moment. Sit on your own shoulder, so to speak, and watch yourself enjoy it." I learned that from Eddie Albert.

It might be, though, that the best advice I ever had came from a small, round, odd little man named Charles

F. Frohman. When C. F. sat in his Gothic office in the Empire Theater Building in New York, he would slip off his Congress gaiters and his feet would dangle two inches from the floor. When he talked, he walked up and down, fast, jabbing with a pudgy finger, nodding, barking, leaving sentences trailing behind him tangled up and knotted. He considered saying "Good morning" a waste of time. He ignored time, never carrying a watch. He ignored money, too, never carrying any. His friends or his aides had to slip him bills so he could pay headwaiters.

He gave me advice about all kinds of things—including what amounted to a ban, an interdiction, against marrying Flo Ziegfeld, to which I paid no attention. He said this about plays:

"Americans love to see women triumph, triumph over men.

"You have to make each person in the audience believe something. He has to believe that he could save the situation, prevent a tragedy, or help a likable thief escape if he could just step over the footlights and cry out."

Once he made a suggestion to the great, and fierce, Mrs. Patrick Campbell. Mrs. Campbell turned on him and said:

"Pardon me, Mr. Frohman, but you forget that I am an artist."

"I'll keep your secret," Frohman snapped.

Once when I was rehearsing *The Mind the Paint Girl,*

by Sir Arthur Wing Pinero, Mr. Frohman suggested that I wasn't reading my lines correctly. This angered me because I was always proud of knowing my lines letter-perfect, and I knew these lines.

"I do know my lines," I argued.

"I don't doubt it, Billie," C. F. said. "But you don't seem to know Pinero's."

It was Frohman who advised Barrie to become a playwright. Up to 1896, Barrie had written those wonderful novels, *My Lady Nicotine*, *A Window in Thrums*, and *The Little Minister*, but he had never thought of himself as a dramatist. Frohman turned him into one, and I would give a large prize to know precisely how he argued that knobby-headed, sentimental little Scot into doing it. I asked, but the only answer I got was:

"Sent him cables."

Once when I had a problem in one of Frohman's plays —some trouble about a Canadian accent, which I wasn't getting just right—C. F. gave me this advice:

"Consult an expert. Mind, now: when you consult an expert, do *exactly* what he tells you to do."

I sought a voice coach, from Montreal, and learned that my British accent wasn't Canadian at all. I did *exactly* what he said and pleased Frohman.

I have remembered that advice all my life, used it, and have gradually come to understand that it was a good deal deeper than casual.

One time a young writer, a talented fellow, most attractive, came to me with a problem he had with a story he was writing. I wanted to help but I couldn't. It wasn't the kind of story I know anything about, and besides, I don't write stories. So I said, "Why don't you see Malcolm Gregory, who is the best man in the world at this kind of thing, and do what he says?"

My young friend did see Mr. Gregory, who was busy but gave up his time and helped him. The young writer sold his story and went back to thank Malcolm Gregory.

"You saved me," he said. "And the reason was, I did exactly as you told me."

Malcolm laughed.

"Tell you something, young feller," he said. "I wouldn't have done that story the way I told you to do it. I would have taken a short cut here and there. The fact is, I'm lazy. But I told you the *best* way to do it. So what happened was, you wrote a better story than I would have written."

Ever since then, when I've wanted advice, I've gone to experts, not to family, friends, or the man on the street. Family and friends always give you what they know you want: approval. This is nine times out of ten exactly what you don't need.

Don't ask the man on the street for directions. Ask the man in the filling station. He has a map.

Don't seek out any old expert. Seek out the best possible expert in the field you're interested in and ask him, or her. If he or she won't be bothered with you, find another expert. Then do what you're told and do it exactly, don't change it, don't leave part of it out, don't mutter, "Oh, she says thus and so but she's exaggerating, I know she doesn't do that herself."

You're right, you know. She doesn't. But she'll tell you how to do it *better* than she does it.

I can prove this theory. When I wanted to hold forth about fashions in this book I went to Renie, who knows more than I do, and when I wanted advice on make-up I went to Max Factor, Jr.

Lionel Barrymore, who worked for Charles F. Frohman too, used to say: "If you want to portray a plumber on stage, go consult a plumber if you are lucky enough to know one. Don't imitate some actor who never knew a plumber."

The best advice I ever had about diet, many years ago, was from a doctor who was outrageously overweight. But he was an expert and he knew it and I knew it and I did *exactly* what he said and benefited.

I think I have it now. The best advice I ever had was to get good advice—*and take it.*

Chapter 11

EASY EXERCISE

I RESENT PIECES in newspapers and magazines that instruct me how to inflate my bosom or flatten my rear. If I am reasonably round here and there that's how I want to keep it. I do not want to balance a book on my head, either. I don't want to stand like a fashion model with my pelvis sprung and my right toe pointed as if I'd broken my ankle. I don't want more muscles than I've got, and I don't want to be told how to kill myself with a set of stunts intended for an acrobat.

If I can't touch my toes without bending my knees,

that's good enough for me. I'll touch them when necessary by exercising my knees.

At the same time, I don't recommend the theory of an actress friend of mine who insists that the best exercise is sitting on a bar stool. She says this keeps her elbows in good condition.

I want to stay elastic—and alive. I hold to the Billie Burke Passive Exercise School, which argues that you certainly have got to keep in shape, old girl, you have got to do something about it, but let's do it in the least painful way possible.

Let's not go leaping about in front of open windows, looking funny and probably catching a cold. Let's not do push-ups and nip-ups, and stretching, straining calisthenics designed for pole vaulters and high jumpers. I was taken to a track meet at UCLA recently and saw the boys warm up by doing the splits and performing other strange feats—only they weren't strange. They were exercises I had just seen suggested for housewives in a woman's magazine.

Actually, I am rather more used to exercise, possibly, than the average woman.

My husband was six feet one and weighed 180 pounds. He used bar bells daily, hefted weights I couldn't pick up, and whenever possible escaped from Broadway to camp, hunt, and fish in Florida or Canada. When we lived at Hastings he used to chin himself five or six times from the branch of a maple tree every morning before he left for town. This is not the usual picture people have of "The Great Glorifier."

Flo started in show business as manager of Eugene Sandow, the big, blond, Austrian strong man, whom he made world-famous. Mr. Sandow wrestled with bears. Once they had to leave San Francisco by boat in a hurry because a dishonest bear "threw" a match to Mr. Sandow, but that is another story. My point is that Flo was interested in muscle tone other than the shape of *Follies* girls and so was I. We both exercised constantly and vigorously. I used bar bells—very light ones, of course—which I learned to hold straight out in front of me while walking around my bedroom. The idea was to "firm up" my arms and shoulders. I also used a parallel bar fixed in a dressing room door. I chinned myself on that.

I was an actress in light comedies—I was the ingénue, the doll, the girl with red hair in the height of fashion; but I might have become a chunk if I had not dieted and exercised.

I followed this program for years. It became not tedious "diet" and "exercise" but a way of life. But this was a vigorous program and I gradually outgrew it, just as a businessman approaching forty outgrows the need for football practice. He keeps in shape, if he values his health, with activities that are more efficient for him than butting heads.

Of course, people who started out as athletes, or who are "good at things," like swimming, tennis, and golf, find it easier later on in life to do what keeps them sturdy and warm and bright of eye. But doctors say that it is hardly ever too late to start a physical program. Some who let themselves slip have begun at seventy or eighty with results so happy that they feel years younger. Some young people of merely thirty are actually in worse condition than their elders by forty years. It's never too late or too soon.

Here are some points:

It's weak muscles that make you droop, make your carriage slump, and which contribute as much as anything else to making you look older and feel older. Years have nothing to do with slackening muscles. It is simply lack of exercise that weakens muscles. The old principle of "what we don't use we lose" stands good here.

All actresses know about correct posture—but we're not going into diagrams and things like that here. Actresses know that they act with their bodies as much, maybe more, than they do with their faces or their voices. We droop to look lazy and tired. We slump, with caved-in chests, to look old. We totter on apparently weak legs to appear ancient. So what is your stance? It won't be firm and young unless you have some muscles in good condition to hold you up.

They don't have to be big muscles—that is one of the reasons why I invented the Billie Burke Passive Exercise School. But they have to be elastic muscles. Loss of elasticity is what creates what we call "old age."

Here are three things we all should do:

Move every joint and contract every muscle every day—but not until it hurts.

Set up a routine. Take your exercises at the same time every day. The best times are in the morning, first thing, and at night, last thing.

Keep a record. If you show a drop in ability, don't worry at first, this may not be permanent, probably isn't. But if you show any steady decline, see your doctor.

You should have a physical checkup and consult your own doctor before you undertake *any* course of exercise, including the simple ones I am going to recommend. Remember that the average person like you and me does not need the workouts that professional athletes or growing boys demand. One of the best forms of exercise is to have a growing boy around the house. Picking up after him will do wonders for your back.

Here are some simple ideas that won't hurt you and will do you good, but see your doctor anyway:

The Walking-Breathing Stroll—Everybody recommends walking as the best of all exercises. Everybody *does* walk—how many miles a day do you suppose a housewife covers daily in the mere performance of her chores? She covers many miles, but this isn't exercise. Salesmen walk. Office workers walk. It doesn't count. It all depends on how you walk, and here is a good way, attributed to Gene Tunney:

Begin by walking a half mile—no more, take it easy—at about three miles an hour.

Breathe *in* as you take your first step. Breathe *out* with your next. Repeat this for twenty steps.

When you have done that (for twenty steps) breathe *in* for the next *two* steps, *out* for the next *two* steps. That is, breathe in ten times and out ten times for the next forty steps.

Then increase the cycle so that you breathe *in* and *out* every three steps, and do that ten times for sixty steps.

When you finish that, increase the pace: *in* and *out* for three steps, four, five, six, seven, eight, nine and ten.

Out of breath anywhere along the line? Then slow down. If you find you can't comfortably sustain respiration for five steps, don't go farther until you are ready to do it with ease.

I'm not trying to make a cross-country runner out of you, just to show a good way to get air in the lungs. Do it without strain.

Here are some more exercises:

The Trick with the Shot Bags—Make two small light-weight canvas bags four and one-half inches by seven and one-half inches in size, similar to beanbags children used to play with. Make them of sturdy material because, instead of beans, you put small buckshot in them. Five pounds in each bag. You will be able to buy this at your local sporting goods store or they will order it for you. Get the very small size, eight or nine, because this will make the bags easier to manage for exercising. The cost is about thirty-five cents a pound if you buy in ten-pound lots.

If you think five pounds in each hand is too heavy for you, start out with lighter ones, but I started out with five pounds in each bag and found it easily manageable. The same rule applies in using the shot bags for exercise. Do not overdo at first; avoid fatigue.

I find them most useful in several exercises for muscle toning. You can use a garter elastic and slip them on your feet and lie flat on your back in bed, if you want to pamper yourself and not get down on the floor. Start out just lifting the legs two or three times with the weights attached—wonderful for the leg muscles. Begin with just one bag resting on the diaphragm and do deep breathing exercises—a minute or two to start with. Before many days go by you will find that you can manage two, and your diaphragm muscles will be wonderfully strengthened. Ask your doctor about this before you try it.

The Sewing Machine Exercise—Here is a much milder form of workout, easy, simple, and fun because you can do something else, like reading or writing letters, at the same time, and still feel smug because you are taking your exercise.

Use an old-fashioned treadle sewing machine. You do not have to do any sewing. Sit at this and treadle away, varying your speed and varying the time to suit your fatigue, and you will soon discover that you are doing wonders for your leg and feet muscles. This is excellent for circulation.

Many families own old machines, no longer used, which they'll be glad to give you. But sewing machine shops also have them. Having converted so many old-type machines to electricity, they'll be glad to sell you, cheap, their leftover treadles and wheels.

More about Walking and Standing—I've noticed, as you have, that so many women tend to walk with their legs a bit too far apart. This is a graceless way of locomotion. Mr. Ziegfeld abominated the practice and used to train his show girls by having them walk a straight chalk line, one foot before the other. The legs should move closely enough together so that the knees just graze in passing.

Vasiliu

When you straddle you leave a double line of foot-prints, which proves you are waddling. And this broad-ens you because it builds up muscles exactly where you don't want 'em.

Try this:

Stand against a wall or door with your feet together

and your heels an inch or so from the wall. Thrust your shoulders back against the wall, so that your weight is supported there. Now you can reach down and feel the muscles from the back of your hip and the large tendons to your knees. You may be surprised to discover how large they are. They need elasticity, exercise, and this "passive" way—merely standing against a wall—is actually a wonderful way to stretch and use them. Mind—no strain.

Now (you're still standing against the wall) contract your rear muscles. You'll feel them pulling down the back of your pelvis. This tilts the front of the pelvis slightly up, and helps straighten the curves of your spinal column.

And this happens: Your abdomen is pulled back and your chest and neck muscles are pulled straight. Your round shoulders are now gone.

All of this without moving or taking a step—but don't discount it. It's exercise.

You should do this daily, several times. Practice it. When you get the hang of it (it may take a few days for you to feel and experience what is happening) you will be standing *right*. This is not the same thing at all as assuming your posture is "correct" merely because you have sucked in your belly and stuck out your chest.

Now: When you have done these things a few times against the wall, step out. Walk. You'll automatically walk with good, correct posture, and you'll feel better, freer, easier.

Lift your feet, with a free swing forward at hips, knees, and ankles. *Put your foot down as an entire object.* Do NOT stab the floor or the sidewalk with your heels. Come down on your heels and on the balls of your feet at the same time.

The next time you see the magnificent Marlene Dietrich on the screen or on television, take a good, careful look. See how she walks in a single track, never waddling. Watch her free swing. Notice her shoulders, easily back. And you can truthfully say: "I walk exactly like Marlene Dietrich."

Other Exercises—They're all good, of course, in moderation or with zeal, according to how you feel, what you're capable of, and what your doctor tells you you can do or need to do.

Play golf—by all means, if you can afford it, but not eighteen holes every other Sunday. This may merely exhaust you. Play every day if you can. Or make shots at a driving range.

Tennis, anyone? Swimming? Bowling? Of course. But remember that these sports, while rewarding and good for everybody, tend to develop special muscles instead of all the muscles. And don't take them up overnight unless you have first put yourself in condition with some "approach" exercises such as the ones we have been talking about, the "passive exercises."

Dancing? Any time I'm lucky enough to get asked, especially square dancing, so popular now and so much fun. But be warned there too. Square dancing can be pretty vigorous and an entire evening of it will give you very tired legs indeed. Work up to it, then have a ball.

To sum up:

1. The ugliest woman of all can be attractive—at least, she can certainly make an entrance—if she has good carriage.

2. Take it easy, take it easy, take it easy. NEVER approach exhaustion.

3. Remember that weak muscles make you look older, but weak muscles are not the result of age; they are the result of laziness.

4. I'm not a doctor. I'm sure what I've put down is harmless, but don't, please, blindly accept *anybody's* set of exercises as good for you until you have had expert counsel.

5. Do *something*. Let's not just sit and sag.

Chapter 12

THEY

I AM SICK and tired of the simpering theory that all men are really just little boys at heart. An adult male human is no more an infant than a stag is a fawn, or a lion is a cub, or a stallion is a colt, and the woman who assumes that she can operate a man like a child is hastening toward a shocking and probably painful surprise.

But the American husband in all his majesty is singularly backward in a number of intellectual situations. There are times when a young wife is bound to conclude that the brilliant, witty, intelligent, and adoring fellow she thought she married is either a fraud or a medium-rare moron.

For instance:

1. *They* do not comprehend simple English. Consider this:

While a husband reads Red Smith and reorganizes the Dodgers, a wife moves in quick starts and stops between the kitchen, the living room, the back bathroom, and the den. Her movements are vital to the comfort and survival of the household. She talks while she moves. She says:

"What's-her-name said, you know, I *mean*. The little place on the other corner where I go. Her name's I forget, is it O.K.? and it'll be pressed, so all right? It was just a sniffle, pot roast, and on your way home the Vermouth who'll drive? Now *don't* forget because it's Friday it is Friday isn't it and the Carmichaels."

A husbandly response to this is, "Of course, dear," and this deceives many fine women. The fact is that the poor man, who may be so bright that he can make thousands of dollars a week as a corporation lawyer, is incapable of understanding any of the important things he has just been told. Another woman would not only comprehend but would have said eight important things herself.

But when you instruct or inform a man you have to put thoughts into basic statements, one at a time, and you have to hold still. A woman in motion confuses a man. She comes through to him as a blur and he gets the notion that there are too many women around for him to cope with. He blanks out.

You have to translate for him like this:

"Margaret, who runs the beauty parlor on the corner, wants me to have a henna rinse tomorrow. Do you approve?"

And:

"Your suit is pressed for the party and I'll pick it up as usual."

And:

"As you remember, dear, junior had a cold this morning, but it was just a sniffle, so it's all right if we get a baby sitter and go to that party."

And:

"We are having pot roast for dinner."

And:

"Pick up a bottle of Vermouth on your way home because the Carmichaels are stopping by for cocktails before we go to the party."

And:

"The date of the party is *Friday* night, so don't forget it, and please come home early."

You can tell a husband these fine things in about twenty-two seconds, saving his time and yours, but he will forget the Vermouth, the party, and the Carmichaels, and swear you never mentioned one of them. The only solution is to get his full attention, with blows if necessary, and impregnate him with one fact at a time. Then rehearse him and ask questions.

2. *Their* friends are loyal, upstanding, intellectual, and admirable. This includes the engineer who plays bum poker, the sales manager who can't pass a bar without a refill, the old college chum who has run through the inheritances of five wives, and several gentlemen of indeterminate occupation who seem to spend all their time urging your husband to go fishing. They are loyal, intellectual, and admirable. The Wellesley graduates with whom you play bridge on odd Tuesdays are frivolous gossips who ought to stay home.

Just understand this and don't forget it. It is part of the Constitution of the United States, which was written by men.

3. *They* run their offices with the organized precision of electric clocks and why can't you run your house that way? The fact that they sometimes come home suffering from exhaustion, boss-phobia, and dismissal notices is not relevant. Once upon a time there was a wife who *did* run her house with the organized precision of an electric clock. Everybody hated her and her husband ran away with a girl who couldn't tell time.

4. *They* are authorities on women's styles, which means that your neckline is too low and your skirts are too high. Don't question this superior knowledge. *Au contraire*, brag about it, especially in public, and you may be pleased by the new dresses you get.

5. *They* never have minor illnesses. Their illnesses are lethal. Their pains are the most anguished sufferings known to medical science and can be authenticated by the Mayo Clinic. Your ailments are psychosomatic.

6. *They* never gossip. *You* gossip. They know you do because they listen with attention. Most men are fair about this, though, and will let you listen to them, although what they say is not gossip. It is news.

7. *They* know how to treat headwaiters and how to order a dinner, *you* don't. And they may just be right about this, having enjoyed more coffee breaks, business luncheons, and expense account dinners than their wives. So be demure and let them order for you. It's not only good form but it's profitable: They may forget they're not on an expense account.

8. *They* had a harder day than you did. You may have swabbed the kitchen floor, argued with eight bill collectors, minded a baby with whooping cough, or you may have *had* a baby. They may have attended a Shriners' convention in Las Vegas. But they had a harder day than you did. Let them get that out of their systems first

and they may gallantly take you dancing if you can convince them it's their own idea.

9. *They* know the way. No matter how lost and late you are on a country road in New Jersey or a baffling freeway in Los Angeles, never force them to "ask that man." That man just may get you lost even more desperately than you are already, and if that's going to happen, it's better, isn't it, to be lost with your own feller and in a good mood?

10. *They* can fix it. Never offer advice about the repair of a vacuum cleaner, garbage disposal, or tricycle or you'll find yourself with a repair job on your hands. If you do it well, they'll hate you. If you mess it up, they'll scold you. Best tactic: If your man's a good fixer, let him alone. If he isn't so handy, smuggle in an expert and say nothing.

11. *They* run their businesses, the nation, the world commerce on credit. But your charge accounts are not credit, they are frivolous and unnecessary spending calculated to inspire bankruptcy. There is only one way to handle this problem with tact and common sense: Be thrifty and sneaky.

12. *They* think that the best time to rumple, kiss, and pat a girl is exactly when she's just finished a full, ready-to-go-out-and-knock-'em-dead job of lipstick, hairdo, powder puff, and costume. She considers herself as untouchable as a freshly painted water color and tends to

resist. The best advice I can offer you, my lucky girl, is this: Don't be a little idiot.

These are a few of the things that every young girl should know about the management of those surprising people, men. It isn't enough to look as fresh as a Cannon towel ad or to run a tidy house, or to meet with smiles the small and large emergencies of man and woman living together. You also have to recognize these and other limitations of the male.

The foregoing articles of faith are true, tested, tried, and proved. Keep them in mind and you'll be happier. Most important, I think, is No. 1. If you forget all the rest, at least do practice speaking in simple, completed sentences. Stand still and say what you mean. You may delight a husband with the impression that for the first time in his life he is beginning to understand at least one woman.

Chapter 13

SOMETHING GOOD TO EAT

THE ZIEGFELD MENUS at Hastings and Palm Beach were oversized and so was the cook. Her name was Delia. Delia was Irish, hot-tempered, and fat. She waged war with tradesmen, grocers, and butchers under the impression that they were all rascals out to cheat her. Once I saw her throw a leg of lamb at a butcher boy along with a string of Gaelic curses that must have turned him purple. She liked plump people and her life's ambition was to keep all members of the family round. It may have been a good thing that we eventually went bankrupt and could not afford Delia.

But she nourished us magnificently, with no technicalities about counting calories.

Delia's dinners began with a soup or seafood cocktail, followed by filet of sole followed by salad with cheese sticks, depending on the appetizer; next a roast—beef, lamb, veal, or chicken; green vegetables and potatoes followed by dessert, a chocolate soufflé, rice pudding, bread pudding, or brown Betty; then fresh fruit, nuts, demitasse and mints and some tidbit of candy.

Luncheons might consist of jellied consommé, cold poached eggs *en gelée*, crab filled with cold cooked marinated vegetables, biscuit tortoni, or a parfait.

In Florida almost every meal started with stone crabs or crawfish, whether it was a party or not.

It's pretty thoroughly established nowadays that most (at any rate, a great many) ailments of the human race

asilio

are traceable to malnutrition—which does NOT mean eating too little. As often as not the undernourished are the very ones who consume quantities of the wrong food. Calorie counters are sometimes among the worst offenders. Rich as they were, the Ziegfeld menus were packed with vitamins. Our guests may have been overfed but they were well nourished.

Flo's ideas about dinner parties were sometimes distressing to both his cook and his wife. Once when we had a house on Jungle Road in Palm Beach and had invited a number of formal people from London and Philadelphia, he ignored what I had planned and had fifty pounds of corned beef with yellow turnips and Irish potatoes prepared by Dinty Moore in New York and flown down steaming hot. I was embarrassed by this hearty food for delicate guests, but they sniffed, fell to, and ate so much that some of the ladies had to be assisted to their cars.

Meantime, Flo was always on a diet. He was faithful about it, never missing a bite. He ate the diet first, then Delia's dinner. I dieted too. We drank gallons of acidophilus milk and dosed ourselves with large glasses of hot water and lemon juice before breakfast. Flo also believed that a few drops of iodine were good for everybody in drinking water. He prowled the dining room like a Borgia, putting iodine in water glasses with an eye dropper. I recall one party attended by Mary and Will

Rogers, George Gershwin, Eddie Cantor, Ray Bolger, Gene Buck, Bernard Sobel, Joseph Urban, Alfred Lunt, Lynn Fontanne, Jerome Kern, and others, at which no water was drunk by anybody.

As I've confessed, I never became a fine cook. But in recent years I have learned some things about food and its preparation and I do indeed have my own kitchen, and use it every day, and survive. I have some definite, simple ideas about nourishment that I think are good and practical. We'll come to them in a moment. Meantime, for fun and good eating, I have some of Delia's recipes I want to pass on. They are not for anybody on a diet. Here:

STUFFED EGGPLANT

1 eggplant, scooped out (not too close to edge), sliced
  lengthwise
1 small onion, chopped fine
½ green pepper chopped fine
1 cup bread crumbs
3 slices bacon chopped fine after frying
1 tomato chopped
pepper and salt to taste
2 tablespoons butter
dash of paprika

Melt butter in pan, add onion and pepper, next eggplant, let cook slowly, add bacon, tomato, seasonings and part of bread crumbs, reserving some to cover eggplant. Pour mixture into shell, cover with crumbs, dot with small pieces of butter, cook till nicely browned. Add chicken or lamb slices if you have them.

STUFFED FRANKFURTERS

4 large franks cut lengthwise one-half through. Spread one side with mustard.

Mince a small green pepper, a slice of onion, a few sprigs of parsley and a small heart of celery. Chop together fine, sauté in two spoons of melted butter, cook till slightly brown, add ⅓ cup fresh bread crumbs, mix and add pinch of Bell's poultry seasoning. Stuff franks and fold up. Roll in bacon strips, fasten with toothpicks. Put in baking pan, roast till bacon is brown on all sides. If any dressing is left, cook in pan with franks. Creamed or mashed potatoes should accompany this dish.

SHANKS OF LAMB POT-ROASTED

2 shanks of lamb cracked once. Dredge lightly in flour, pepper and salt. Brown in butter or bacon fat, turning till well browned. In thick-bottomed pot with tight lid, add bay leaf, bunch small carrots, a few stalks of celery, leaves and all, 6 small white onions; let vegetables cook before adding 1 cup boiling water. Cover, let simmer 1½ hours. Add few small potatoes, cook for ½ hour; remove meat, skim fat, make gravy. A tsp. of curry powder added to gravy makes this delicious, if you like curry!

GRANDMOTHER'S HERRING SALAD

(Ziegfeld, that is)

Soak 10 salt herring in cold water 5 or 6 hours. Dry fish. Take same weight of cooked veal, potatoes, beets, apples. 3 pickled cukes—cut in cubes

Mix 2 tbsp. of vinegar
    2 tbsp. of olive oil
    ½ cup claret or white wine
    little sugar
    beet juice
Put dressing over salad—let stand 12 hours.

Patricia, who found this old recipe for me, says she has never tried it herself. She says she is appalled. It was one of Flo's favorites.

SHRIMP NEWBURG (Delia)

Melt ½ cube butter, must be butter, add salt, pepper, paprika, small or large shrimp, sauté till they curl, add some flour, rich cream till desired thickness of sauce, ¼ cup of sherry or to your taste, serve with rice. (4042 calories, but oh how good it is!)

I know, and your own doctor will be glad to tell you, probably at length, that most of us past forty tend to put on too much weight. We overeat as a compulsive habit, seeking satisfactions in the face of worry and frustration. We get fat—and undernourished. Then we undernourish ourselves more with some new and drastic diet and lose a few temporary pounds, meantime putting ourselves in grave danger of illness.

More and more people in my circle of friends, in television, pictures and radio, eat wonder foods for which they claim miracles. These include blackstrap molasses,

whole wheat germ, gelatin, lecithin, yogurt, and brewer's
yeast. These are good, but they are not recommended to
cure any specific disorder, and, except for the lecithin,
they are not new. I've heard about them all my life. It's
best to ask your doctor about these things—you may or
you may not need them.

Our best of all possible bets, I'm convinced, is to avoid
diets (except under medical supervision) and to do something about GOOD NUTRITION. Health food stores are now
opening up in every community. There you can buy
unprocessed foods in great variety. Many of these stores
sell fresh fruits and vegetables in season from farms
where they are grown in soil free of commercial fer-
tilizer. They are more expensive, of course, than the
supermarket products, but the difference is so good for
you and so delicious.

My plan, which I follow except when my doctor has
other plans, is to eat plenty of Nature's freshest foods,
natural foods, containing the mightiest provisions for
maintaining happiness and health. They are high in protein and low in carbohydrates, with enough fat to sustain
energy. But please note carefully that this plan is not for
anybody with some specific ailment requiring a low-fat
diet, or a salt-free or high-starch diet. This is for those of
us who want to keep up our pep and the youthful elasticity of our bodies, along with a bit of easy exercise.

Except for the glass of liquid gelatin with each meal

there is nothing unusual here except, I hope, common sense. This is a pretty rare thing, though, with most of us when we sit down to eat.

Here is a basic menu pattern:

BREAKFAST
Half grapefruit or small orange, sectioned
Stewed prunes or figs (4 prunes, 2 tbsp. juice)
1 glass milk
1 glass gelatin drink
Bacon or ham with egg
1 slice buttered toast
Coffee or tea

LUNCHEON
Broiled liver
Mixed green salad
1 glass milk
1 glass gelatin drink
1 slice whole grain bread with butter
Dessert

DINNER
1 cup clear soup
Roast, fish or fowl (8 oz.)
2 hot vegetables, one yellow
Green salad
1 glass milk
1 glass gelatin drink
Dessert

No cook I, but this food plan is so simple that I manage it very well.

Once a week the woman who cleans my little house prepares a large pot of soup stock and roasts a small beef roast or leg of lamb. She freezes a pound of raw liver. Sometimes she simmers and spices a fresh tongue and leaves it in its rich juice in a covered casserole in the refrigerator.

I get along with a minimum of fuss. Small quantities of fresh fruit, vegetables and greens are delivered daily, along with chops, steak, fish or poultry I plan to have.

A small General Electric easy-to-clean broiler and two attractive one-quart stainless-steel copper-bottom pots with tight, heavy lids are practically the only equipment I use.

I have a little shelf of assorted spices marketed by the Spice Island Co., vegetable salt, coarse ground pepper, ground parsley, paprika, rosemary, and basil. I have fun and adventure with them.

Here are some tips.

Vegetables

1. Buy only the freshest vegetables available in your local markets. Wash thoroughly but as quickly as possible. Never soak in water because this destroys much of the minerals and water-soluble vitamins. Dry and store in the refrigerator until ready to use.

2. Starchy vegetables such as potatoes and yams

should be served no more than once a week; bake or steam in the jackets to preserve the minerals.

3. To conserve the nutritive value of vegetables and bring out their flavor they should be cooked rapidly in very little water or in a tightly closed pot. They should be cooked just to the point of tenderness and salted *after* cooking.

4. Use frozen vegetables when the fresh are of poor quality.

5. For interest and taste appeal, experiment with seasonings of parsley, chives, celery, chopped onion, bell pepper diced, and spices.

Meat

1. Buy only government-inspected meat.

2. Use glandular or organ meats such as liver, kidney, brain, tongue, and sweetbreads as one-third the necessary protein.

3. Do not fry meats. Steaks, chops, and ground meat patties should be broiled and served rare.

4. Ground meat should be used as soon as possible after grinding.

5. Use moderate heat for roasting meat, and salt when nearly done.

6. Simmer tougher cuts of meat over *low* heat.

7. Fish and poultry should be served often.

Milk and Dairy Products

1. Serve one glass of milk with each meal.
2. Use unprocessed cheese.

Eggs

1. Buy only first quality.
2. Do not fry. Vary the cooking of breakfast eggs to avoid monotony. Experiment with seasonings.

Bread and Cereals

1. Buy unprocessed, whole-grain cereals. The health food stores in your community have many varieties. Purchase in small quantities and store in a cool place.
2. Use whole-grain, unprocessed flour in all recipes requiring flour, for thickening sauces and gravies and making pastry.
3. If you cannot make bread at home, buy the unprocessed whole-grain varieties sold in health food stores.

Fruits

1. Fresh fruits should be washed immediately, thoroughly, dried, and placed in the refrigerator. Enzymes which destroy the vitamins cannot act when the food is kept chilled.
2. Frozen fruits rather than canned should be used.

Desserts

1. Sugar content should be cut to the minimum. Use unpasteurized honey or unsulphured molasses in place of refined sugar.

2. Serve simple custards, puddings or fresh fruits in season. Servings should be small, especially of the fruits, which are high in carbohydrates.

3. No candies.

Be sure you incorporate in your menus the foods that contain the complete basic proteins.

We all know that large amounts of protein are found in the meat of fish and animals. But most of us do not know that liver, kidneys, tongue, pancreas, and other organs and glands of fish and animals contain the most complete protein. Serve these at least two or three times each week.

Gelatin, a hydrophilic colloid, should be used as a regular part of every meal because it is not only high in protein—no calories—but particularly because it aids materially in the assimilating of one's food. It is most effective if taken hot. Soak one tablespoon of plain gelatin in a cup with sufficient water to cover. Dissolve in a hot liquid such as soup, hot water with fruit flavoring, or hot water in which a beef cube has been dissolved. Serve this with each meal.

LIVER

Have your meat man slice young beef liver three-quarters to one-inch thick. Broil brown on both sides, but have it pink and juicy inside. Serve with broiled bacon and tomatoes. Wonderful and oh! so good for you.

BRAINS

Wash brains in cold water, remove membranes, rinse thoroughly. Parboil. Drain. Sauté gently in butter until golden brown. Add four eggs well beaten with two tablespoons milk. Scramble lightly, add seasoning and chopped parsley. Serve immediately.

SWEETBREADS

Soak fresh sweetbreads in cold water with one tablespoon of vinegar for half an hour. Parboil gently for twenty minutes. Remove membranes when cool. When thus prepared, sauté lightly in butter, or make a medium white sauce with cornstarch, cover with buttered crumbs, bake until heated through in the oven.

KIDNEYS

Trim, cut kidneys in half, remove white tubes, and soak in salted water for an hour. Use any favorite kidney recipe of your own or try the following:

STEAK AND KIDNEY PIE

One beef kidney prepared as above, cut into cubes. Place in a kettle of cold water, bring to a boil, discard water and repeat a second time. Meanwhile, cut one pound of steak into 1¼-inch cubes, dredge with whole-wheat flour, season with salt and pepper, brown in heavy iron kettle in ¼ cup butter or bacon drippings. Add chopped onion, one teaspoon Worcestershire sauce, cover with cold water, add kidneys, and simmer gently about two hours. Add liquid as needed, and stir to prevent sticking. Pour into casserole, top with a flaky crust made of whole-wheat pastry flour, bake quickly and serve very hot.

HEART

Baked Stuffed Heart: Cut out tough fibers and wash thoroughly in cold water. Simmer for two hours in salted water. Prepare a bread stuffing, stuff the boiled heart and skewer together. Roll in whole-wheat flour, brown in bacon fat, place in covered casserole. Add a small amount of water to pan in which heart was browned, pour it over the heart, and bake slowly in moderate oven until tender, about an hour and a half.

TRIPE

Select pickled or fresh tripe which has already been cooked, or simmer uncooked tripe, thoroughly washed, for six hours or until tender. Let cool in broth. Cut prepared tripe into inch squares, add onions, carrots, celery, bay leaf, peppercorns, a tablespoon of Worcestershire sauce, and simmer about 25 minutes.

FISH CHOWDER

This is a New England type fish chowder which is easy to prepare and should be the main dish at luncheon or supper. Anne Enlows, the well-known home economist, served it at her home and gave me the recipe. This will serve two generously.

1 pound boned whitefish	1 package frozen mixed
3 slices bacon	vegetables
1 cupful diced onion	1 quart (4 cupfuls) water
2 small potatoes (cooked)	salt, pepper and seasoning
1 cupful diced celery	2 tbsp. flour
	1 cupful whole milk

Clean the fish and wash it well. (My fish market sells chunks of boneless whitefish cut especially for chowder.) Add to the cold water, bring slowly to boiling point, and simmer until the fish is tender—about thirty minutes. Do not overcook. Then remove the fish. In the meantime, fry the cut-up bacon until it is light gold. Do not brown. Add onions and simmer until they are tender but do not change color. Add bacon, onions, celery, and mixed vegetables to the fish liquor, season, and cook for about ten minutes. Thicken. Then add the diced potatoes and chunks of cooked fish. Just before serving add milk, a tablespoonful of butter, and a generous amount of chopped parsley. When done, the chowder should be thick with fish and vegetables.

Serve with toasted strips of homemade whole-wheat bread and a tossed green salad and you have a perfect combination.

WHOLE WHEAT BREAD

Here is a recipe for bread made from whole wheat and whole-grain cereals. It has a wonderful nutlike flavor you will not find in any ordinary bread:

2 cups milk	2 yeast cakes
⅓ cup butter	5½ cups unsifted whole-
1 tablespoon salt	wheat flour
½ cup blackstrap molasses or unprocessed honey	

For variety and really fine flavor, two cups of the flour may be replaced with two cups of *cooked* unprocessed whole-grain cereal. There is a Seven Grain Cereal made by the El Molino Mills in California sold at most health food stores. It is a combination of soya, wheat, corn, barley, oats, rye, and rice bran. You may vary the cereal according to preference of flavor.

Heat milk to simmer. Remove from stove and put

shortening, salt, and molasses (or honey) into milk and pour into large mixing bowl. Cool to LUKEWARM.

Dissolve yeast in ⅓ cup lukewarm water. To hasten yeast action, add ½ teaspoon honey. Add dissolved yeast to mixture in bowl.

Add 3 cups flour, stir 8 minutes with electric mixer at low speed; or, 300 strokes by hand. Add 2½ cups flour or cereal mixture and stir well.

Turn dough onto a lightly floured board. Grease your hands with melted shortening to make handling easier. Knead dough by folding it toward you, then pushing away from you with the heel of the hand. Turn the dough as you work it. These two actions are all there is to kneading. Repeat until the dough is smooth and elastic. It should be light enough so you can hold it in your hand a few seconds without sticking.

Knead in more flour if necessary. About fifteen minutes of kneading will produce bread of good, smooth texture.

Place in a well-oiled bowl, cover with towel and set in a warm place to rise until it is double in bulk. (85 degrees F. for about an hour.)

While still in the bowl, punch down to original size and let rise again.

Turn onto a lightly floured board and cut dough in two with a sharp knife. Make into two balls. Flatten out dough and punch all air out with closed fists. Fold dough lengthwise. Flatten again, then stretch to lengthen it. Fold into three and press firmly together, sealing the edges. Form into a roll and place in oiled bread pan, sealed edge down. Cover with a towel and let rise again until dough begins to lift the towel.

Place to bake in 375 degree F. preheated oven for one hour or until golden brown. Remove from pans and place on rack to cool. If soft crust is desired brush with cream or soft butter.

This bread will fetch the grandchildren around and their parents cannot complain that you are feeding them improperly. A batch in the oven is so savory that you can make a satisfactory aromatic impact on an entire neighborhood. It's great with honey. It's crunchy and delicious toasted. Men like it, and Southern boys, who prefer it hot, are likely to sing "Dixie" for you.

SOUP

Make a large kettle of soup stock once a week. Inexpensive cuts of meat are best because they have more flavor and contain more nourishment. Use plenty of bone, such as shank and knuckle, which should be cracked and split by the butcher. Cut the meat and marrow from the bone and brown in a little suet. Cover with cold water and let stand for an hour before cooking. Add ¼ cup vinegar and salt to flavor. Simmer gently for four hours or until meat falls from the bone, skimming about every thirty minutes. Then add ½ cup diced celery and leaves, and 1 cup each diced carrot and onion. Simmer for an hour longer. Strain, cool, remove the fat and clarify the stock.

To clear soup stock, mix the whites of two eggs with the crushed shells and two tablespoons cold water. Add to the strained broth and stir and boil for three minutes. Then reduce the heat and simmer for ten minutes, and re-strain. When cool, store the broth in the refrigerator.

With vegetables and seasonings you can make many varieties of soups. Serve at least once a day. Starting a meal with a soup stimulates the gastric juices and encourages better digestion.

THE BILLIE BURKE COCKTAIL

I can't make a Martini, or even an acceptable whisky-and-soda for a gentleman caller, but there is one cocktail I do know how to prepare and here it is:

One of the best midmorning or midafternoon pickups for energy and over-all well-being is the liver tomato juice cocktail. Wash young beef liver in cold water and dry on paper towel. Remove skin and tough fibers with a very sharp knife. Freeze. When you are ready to make your cocktail, grate about two tablespoons of the frozen liver, stir it quickly into a glass of cold tomato juice, season well with Worcestershire sauce, horse radish, or any favorite seasoning, salt and pepper, and drink at once.

Be sure to return the liver to freezing compartment immediately after grating. A pound of liver will make a week's supply of cocktails if kept frozen.

This is a stimulant. Anything containing alcohol, no matter how pleasant, is a depressant. Some of my best friends are depressed.

I lunched with a lady of distinction the other day who fussed and worried about what to order. She finally decided on baked avocado with a filling of chicken and mushrooms in rich cream sauce, topped with cheese.

She reassured herself:

"It's simply wonderful the way they do it here, and it's my favorite. Of course, it *does* use up my whole day's allowance of calories, but I shan't eat another *bite* until tomorrow.

"Besides, all I had for breakfast was *black* coffee.

"You know, I don't *dare* put on another pound before Marion's wedding. My 'mother-of-the-bride' dress is a little on the *tight* side, so I just don't dare.

"My dear, there's so much to be done before the wedding! I'm so exhausted sometimes I think I won't be able to make it."

She'll make it, poor darling, somehow. The dress will fit beautifully, even though she looks worn and haggard and *is* exhausted because she didn't eat properly. But this was no time to talk nutrition to her. As soon as that wedding is over I'll have to do a little missionary work.

My friend is an example of what happens to calorie counters when they get a number complex. They take out their little charts and consult them like prayer books every time they order lunch—never realizing that you can go undernourished and lacking energy while you're eating two to three times the calories you should have.

Anna Held, I always remember sadly, that beautiful person, died of anemia as the result of a drastic diet to regain her figure.

But it is never too late (and it certainly can't be too soon) to begin a good eating program. Please remember:

1. Don't diet to lose weight unless you do it under your doctor's orders.

2. It's the proteins that give you energy, the highest specific dynamic action.

3. The carbohydrates I've mentioned are in whole grains, unrefined, the starches of vegetables, and in meats.

4. If you eat correctly, for strength and energy, you will never have to diet. As in proper, easy exercise, eating right should become a way of life, not an imposition.

Anyone for lunch?

Chapter 14

GOING STEADY

WHEN I was a girl—in the morning of Time, somewhere around the Paleozoic Era, according to my grandchildren—the term "going steady" was in use but it didn't mean what it means today. Up to World War II it meant that a girl was spoken for, object matrimony. A steady fellow might hanky-panky around for thirty years avoiding the altar, that's true, but the affair was at least understandable any way it came out.

I never went steady. I was a child of the theater, which may be romantic but never was steady. Young men who took me out fell into three categories: the ones who liked to escort girls, especially actresses, to parties and theaters; the heads-over-heels boys who wanted to get married and who died for love a thousand times over several girls at once; and the bounders (now known as wolves) who had something else in mind.

Mother kept a suspicious eye on all of them. She timed my "dates" as if they were three-minute eggs and questioned my young man as if she were loaning me out at 6 per cent. All this took place in London. We went to "nice" places, danced decorously, and came home in broughams. I never heard of a boy and girl parking in a brougham.

I watched other actresses, a few years older and half a century freer than I, with poignant curiosity when they went out with rich playboy friends. Possibly something went on that I did not know about. I was pretty innocent, although eager to get informed. I thought that holding a young man's hand was thrilling (I wonder if I don't still think so!), and as for kisses, I was under the impression that they were a sure preliminary either to a scandal or a marriage.

Nowadays, girls not only go out with boys at extraordinarily early ages—fourteen and fifteen—but "go steady" with them before their parents even meet these boys. And a going-steady boy and girl do exactly that; they don't go with anybody else.

It seems to me that it was more fun to go out with

several boys, or a lot of them if I could get them, than with just one. The British are more romantic than you might think, in spite of tweeds and monocles and unusually good manners. All girls had young men who protested enduring love. It was gratifying when they announced they'd be suicides by morning if I didn't have them. No one even nicked himself or dipped a toe in the Thames over me, but they enjoyed the threats and so did I. I suppose young men say to young women today: "Babe, I dig you the most. You're my chick, aintcha?"

But I undoubtedly got that all wrong. All generations younger than mine speak languages hard to understand. By the time you have studied and mastered their syntax, they have invented a new language. I learned "square," "hep," and "dig," just as those terms—I think—went out of style. I heard a few days ago two new and rather interesting phrases: "all-time," meaning what used to be expressed by "the most." They mean the same as "napa," if you know what I mean. But I don't use these words. By the time I think I have them in hand, they will be out of favor faster than you can say, "Twenty-three skiddoo."

So, in approaching going steady and all other problems of the young, I find that Grandma should speak her own language, whether it's with an Oklahoma accent or with a slight English accent, like mine. If you try to talk their tongues, your grandchildren will be ashamed of you, will mutter, "Oh, Grannie, you don't understand,"

and if you are embarrassingly wrong they'll be horrified, as if you'd taken up necking in parked cars.

When I became a "young lady" (there's an outworn term; where did the "young ladies" go?), I fell in love with all the right people. I adored a brilliant young man named Winston Churchill, who looked like a redheaded boy and spoke like a young king, but I never let him know it. I pretended to avoid Enrico Caruso, who was much too florid for me, but I led him on a little for fun. I was very much in love with Somerset Maugham, who, if he reads this, will learn that news for the first time.

Mr. Maugham was thirty-six years old when I knew him in New York, in 1910. I starred in his plays—*Mrs. Dot, The Land of Promise* and *Caesar's Wife*—and went out with him often. He was pale and interesting. Eventually, he took me to a ball at the Astor Hotel and led me down the grand stairway straight (and literally) into the arms of Florenz Ziegfeld, Jr.

Before that, after I had been in one of his plays for a year or so, he bought himself a handsome new house in London. He had a charmingly framed little picture of me over the fireplace in the entrance hall. His guests would ask:

"Who is the girl in that picture?"

Maugham would reply:

"Oh, that is the lady who bought me this house."

Witty, I thought. But acting in his comedies and making him some money to buy a house was as close to going steady with Willie Maugham as I got.

The young regard us as dinosauric because we question going steady. They are not on hard ground here. They don't quite understand it themselves. I know some girls and boys who scornfully oppose the custom—there are always mavericks in any society, including the teenage tribes. But many girls think of going steady as the greatest invention since vanilla. Others are hopeful and trembling, willing, but not getting asked. The boys are trapped. I think any up-and-going young man would prefer to play the field. He's not ready at seventeen to practice monogamy. But young women rule the roosters.

Parents I talk to are ambivalent. Fathers of girls snort, grin, and gloom about after leaving the porch light on when daughter has a date. Mothers sneak out and turn the light off. Mothers are coy. They abet the going-steady custom as a social security device and set loaded traps in their refrigerators.

As for the girls, take one who is not related to me but who frequently leans on the door of my sitting room (the young can't stand up today, they have to lean on something). Her name is Amy. She prods me for information about Men. She thinks, because I am an actress, that I know all about Sin and Wickedness and may tell her some perfumed secret. I sponsor this delusion to keep her respect.

Amy went to a high-school dance the other night with the football boy with whom she goes steady.

"Have fun, dear?" I asked. "Get a rush? Dance with lots of boys?"

She gave me that look, the one that means "Here-we-go-again-but-you'll-never-dig-it, old lady."

"It was real neat," she told me patiently. "But I didn't dance with lots of boys. Just with Jim. Of course."

"Every dance with Jim?"

"Naturally." (She may have said "Natch.")

I sympathized. "Were you *stuck*?"

"Stuck" is a my-generation word. The child didn't grasp it at first. It used to be that dancing with one man only, the fellow that brought you, was the ultimate disgrace. It used to be that at Princeton and Yale proms, such a boy who was "stuck" with a girl, even if she was a peach, would wave a dollar bill behind her back as a bribe to some brother to take her off his hands for a few rounds.

"Not 'stuck,' Miss Burke," Amy explained. "Everybody dances every dance with their dates. I mean, you know, well *guy*, you just dance with your own date, of course."

It seems like dull entertainment to me. I wouldn't, for instance, want to dance every dance anywhere all night even with Clark Gable if I was so lucky. Let's take it back to my era: with a Prince of Wales. One of the

Barrymore boys, or their uncle John Drew, or Flo Ziegfeld, might be there, and I would be in a snit if they
didn't want to dance with me. I'd want what we called a
bit of a "rush." It was fun, being cut in on by various
men, like a cake at a picnic.

I explain this to the young but they don't dig me.

They not only dance all evening with the same fellow
but tie him up in every other way possible.

There are mutations. I note that youngsters of thirteen
go steady, too. Chuck, a thirteen-year-old neighbor of
mine, goes steady with a pretty little girl of twelve who
wears braces. He explained this to me. He hollers "Hi!"
in the hall to her and makes faces at her in a civics
class. These attentions establish their going-steadyhood.
Chuck never "dates" his girl. But he talks to her every
night. *She* calls *him* on the telephone and does his Health
and Safety homework for him.

Two kids a little older go steady this way: Albert
takes Alice to all stated high-school functions such as
proms and Boy Scout dances. Otherwise he ignores
Alice, who is content with the arrangement. Something
warmer just might develop here (say by next spring
when the buds bud and the sap rises), but it seems un-
likely. Alice has social security, all she wants now, and I
know as a matter of fact that she has an eye on a senior.

Going steady for real, the full treatment, is what

frightens parents—and possibly with good reason. The process is loaded with protocol and possibilities.

The girl wears the boy's ring, or some other token, according to the clan custom in her community, and goes with no other boy anywhere, not ever. Let's call the boy Bob. Bob is utterly obligated. He has to work hard (as a box boy at a supermarket) in order to afford his girl, who's a real number. Let's call her Nancy.

Bob has to have a car. He can and does borrow the family car on occasion, but this isn't always available. It's better if he has his own. He cannot, of course, be chauffeured on a date by his mother or father one minute past the time his voice changes. So he owns, with a considerable financial boost from his father (called a "loan" but never repaid), a fifth-hand Chevy, Ford, or "Merc." To maintain his "heap" in proper shine for going steady, he has to become an expert mechanic, remove all dents, and do something called "revving up" the engine.

For a dance, he provides a corsage, average price here around $3.50. He pays about $2.50 for his high-school dance ticket. Then he takes Nancy out after the dance and feeds her. I thought that kids went, of course, to some inexpensive malt shop or hamburger joint. They don't. They go to the Sheraton-Huntington in Pasadena, to the Biltmore Bowl in Los Angeles, and to Ernie's in San Francisco. (I'm a little ahead of myself, but not much: Ernie's is where Stanford and Berkeley seniors take sophomore girls after dances.) On the average, a high-school boy taking a high-school girl out—corsage, prom, and after-prom victuals—has to spend at least $18.

I think that this is outrageous all the way around, either in high school or college. It has set the falsest possible standards. The working-his-way-through-school boy, who may be the most attractive and the brightest boy in his class and President of the United States in 1990, cannot afford to take out girls who, as a matter of fact, might much prefer to go with him—even if only for a coke or a walk around the quad. But the poor boy can't date the popular dolls. Custom and going steady decree certain gestures that cost too much money, and he is embarrassed to ask her to forego them.

Just the other day a story appeared in all the papers here which said that in many Midwestern colleges the "proms" and "hops"—they have various names—were being abandoned. These big delightful events which used to be so gay and charming, creating so many gay memories, are being called off because—well, what's the use of spending all that money for a huge ball, a name band, corsages, and food when you're going to dance with the same girl all night? The same girl you have a date with every night? It seems to me that in losing their proms the kids are losing something that's fun and romantic, but at the same time perhaps the young men are coming to their senses.

I suppose the basis for going steady is that a good man is still hard to find. There are not enough "real neat" guys to go around. So a girl achieves social security by tieing up a boy.

What she misses is the rush, the thrill of being sought after, competed for. The young males of my day liked competition. They brought a girl to a dance to show her off, like a prize. They introduced her to their friends, and looked on with pride. After all, she would leave with the boy that fetched her.

A girl can't enjoy an experience like that now. She can't be the belle of the ball. I think this is sad.

She may go through high school knowing only one boy. He may be a nice boy. He may not be the right boy, the one who could really make her eyes dance and her knees weak. But she gets used to him and very often marries him.

And she marries him too soon.

Let's not be statistical, but surely you've read the alarming figures about very young couples, their quick marriages, and their quicker divorces.

Today they want to get married while they're still in college, or while they haven't even finished high school.

Vasiliu

What seems to me so strange about this is that they apparently take it as their right to marry and have babies while being supported and educated.

Sam Levinson discussed this on a television program with Arthur Godfrey and said it all better than I can. I remember a point he made. He said that college boys and girls blackmail their parents with the threat of sexual intercourse before marriage if they are not allowed to have their way.

Please: I don't mean to say that going steady is responsible for all this. But it is part of a confused attitude that people seem to have today.

The old standards we used to respect—or flout—seem to have been put away. A few years ago, there *were* standards, even if they were ignored.

Right now I'm a fuddy-duddy for using two words I'm going to use: "morals" and "ethics." Using those words today is almost as embarrassing as praying in public.

Morals and ethics in 1959 don't seem to be set by the institutions that used to set them. I mean the churches, the teachers, and the parents.

They are set by corporations, which have a say in what kind of wife a man may keep, where he buys his cocktails, and the degree of snobbishness of the suburb he's told to live in.

They are also set by universities, which know an

awful lot about nuclear fission but not too much about good manners.

And by the automobile industry, which has taken the kids out of their homes and into parked cars.

Bernard Shaw used to say that marriage was "the maximum of temptation plus the maximum of opportunity." That's what an automobile is today.

Getting back to the kids, I think they should be required to grow up and earn their privileges before fast marriages and fast cars are handed to them as matters of course.

Parents, instead of teaching sons and daughters by example how to mix Old-fashioneds, how to cheat on expense accounts, how to drive too fast, how to spend too much money, and how to lie about income taxes—parents should wake up and accept their responsibilities.

It may be that going steady is a retreat for boys and girls. They may be huddling in escape from their fathers and mothers.

Chapter 15

DEAR MRS. POST: IS IT ALL RIGHT TO BE POLITE TO A CHILD?

A QUOTATION that may give comfort to bewildered parents and public school principals has been making the rounds recently in newspaper columns. It says this:

Our youth now love luxury—they have bad manners and contempt for authority. They show disrespect for their elders and love idle chatter in place of exercise.

Children are now tyrants—not the servants of the households. They no longer rise when elders enter the room. They contradict their parents, chatter before company, gobble up their food, and tyrannize their teachers.

The tag line to this is that it was said by Socrates in the fifth century before Christ.

I suppose this means that not much progress has been made in spite of all our love and our gentle precepts and the expensive educations we provide for the young. The

boy and girl Greeks who hung around the Olympics and the temples were apparently as wild and impudent as the all-American boys and girls who hang around jukebox joints and theater lobbies. At any rate, we can make excuses: Even the ancient Hellenes, who practically invented modern civilization, had their juvenile delinquents —and their complaining old men. I wonder if Greek parents of 500 B.C. set better examples for their children than we do now.

Did they scream at their kids when they went to buy olive oil and figs in Spartan and Athenian supermarkets? I am about to give up supermarketing in Los Angeles and Beverly Hills because I overhear so many mothers squalling at their tired children: "Shad ap! I'm gonna take your hide off when I getcha home!"

Granted that young people are out of hand (and frequently out of sight, and out of mind, too), I make a modest suggestion. It is that we all might come by politer, more respectful children, if we gave them their own due of respect.

I'd like to see children treated almost as politely as servants. This is difficult to imagine because who has servants any more? But if I had for instance a butler, a cook, and a maid, I'd treat them so gratefully, probably with reverence, that I'd be a polished example of proper manners for all youngsters who came around.

The fact is—and we might as well say it flatly—that the bad manners of parents to children are increasingly, appallingly noticeable. I note this from direct and embarrassed experience. I see parents who expect their offspring to be sweet, charming, and full of "please" and "thank you" but are themselves incredibly rude to their boys and girls, not only at home but in public.

My daughter agrees with me and puts it this way: "There ought to be an underlying, subconscious foundation of good manners and respect at home that in later life would help prevent parents from infringing on their children's privacy."

You know as well as I do of parents who scold their children harshly, anywhere, in front of anybody, for not saying "Beg pardon?" when they want something repeated—but whose reply to anything a child asks is an irritated "Huh?"

The "Huh" puts the child in his place. It is an eloquent grunt indeed. It says in one breath: "I'm too important to be bothered by you, what you asked was undoubtedly silly, go away, don't bother me."

Worse than that, I suppose, because young people can eventually learn at least the techniques of good manners away from home (even in a bar), is the outright betrayal of children's confidences as conversation pieces.

I know a mother who does this constantly. She has a daughter of fourteen (a terrifying, bewildering, dear and groping age) who used to discuss all her misgivings, from sex to algebra, with her mother. She came to her freely, with few reservations, to talk things out. She no longer does. She no longer tells Mother anything. She knows that Mother repeats it all to other mothers over ten o'clock morning coffee or over the bridge table in the evening.

Now the girl is reported to be in "a typical phase of juvenile retreat." According to her mother she "sulks in her room." She "broods." She is "exhibiting tendencies of teen-age revolt against authority."

Is she? Or did she discover that her mother wasn't a gentleman?

Of course we have to teach our children the routines of manners: table manners, thank-you notes, introductions, "I had a nice time at the party, thank you so much," and "How do you do?" instead of "Hi!" when meeting grownups. (Although what's the matter with a well-meant "Hi!" from a small child I don't really know.) We have to teach these things as rules because a child has no way of learning rules unless he *is* taught. I'm being obvious. I know it. But I have a point and I'm told it's good psychology.

The point is that how you act has a direct and immediate effect on how you feel. It's true that if you assume a forced attitude of cheerfulness, you'll actually feel cheerful sooner than if you give way to complaints. This works with good manners, too. Practiced manners, I'm convinced, inspire good will and thoughtfulness. Naturally, the best way to teach them is to demonstrate them —invoke the "rule" only when you need to give the child a peg to hang his memory on. And don't betray him.

I'd say never correct a child's table manners (except unobtrusively and gently) *at* the table. Do it later, and do it out of earshot of guests, even aside from other members of the family. The grubbiest small boy can be expected to appreciate your good manners in protecting him from embarrassment.

In Hollywood I know a screenwriter whose father was a distinguished lawyer. He told me this story:

"I was about ten years old when Father took me with him, one day, to some kind of big conference. Twenty or thirty men—one of them a Superior Court Judge, I believe—sat at a long table and discussed something legal at great length. I think my father took me with him out of pride. He wanted his friends to see what a fine boy he had, so I was washed and polished like a fruit-stand apple. But the meeting was long and dull and I fidgeted, and had to find the bathroom twice, before my father rose to speak. He shoved his chair back from the table and made a long talk.

"I guess what he said was impressive. At any rate, people took notes and looked solemn, and this went on for about an hour.

"By this time I had become a rebel and a father-hater. Why had he stuck me with this stuffy business when I could have been out playing in the dirt? I got even with him. I sneaked up just before he sat down and pulled his chair out from under him.

"He sat down hard on the floor. I know now that it must have hurt terribly. He was a big man. It must have offended his dignity tremendously, too.

"But not one man in that room laughed, or smiled, or even seemed to notice. My father said nothing at all to me. He simply got up, said "Good-by" to the conference, and we went home.

"There he took a hairbrush, took down my pants, and whaled me. I knew I deserved that licking. I would have felt bad, and unpunished, unforgiven, if I hadn't got it.

"I'm grateful to this day that I wasn't thrashed or scolded in front of the gentlemen at the conference. I've always remembered that incident with love and respect for my father. By waiting until he got home to punish me, he not only saved my little dignity but increased his own."

I was amazed to read in *Coronet* not so long ago an article which told me that mommy and daddy are "godlike and awesome" to their preschool-age children. "As parents, you are in every sense of the word god," the article says. "Your motives are mysterious, your methods incomprehensible. You are to be loved—and feared—more than anyone else in the world."

Why, of course, it's true, I suddenly realized. A small child is not a little adult any more than an adult is a large child. So far as the very young are concerned, we larger people belong to a different race of beings. A child can't get it through his head that we were once children ourselves. Indeed, no matter how old and grown up our children are, they still find it just about impossible to conceive of us as having been babies.

Father a baby? Incredible. He was always "Father," and always will be.

The very young look on their parents, of course, as omniscient. They know what's going to happen before it happens—sheer magic, although it merely requires knowing how to tell time and how to read the paper.

We are, they think, utterly virtuous, incapable of lying, of wrongdoing, rudeness, or selfishness. Actually, a small child restrains his natural destructive impulses not so much because you gave him orders as because he needs your love and approval.

There comes a happy time, later, much later—sometimes never—when a son or daughter almost grown up overnight "recognizes" a parent as a human being with forgivable faults, with problems, with quirks, quiddities, bad habits, maybe. And still likes and loves that parent, probably admires him (or her) more than ever.

We are so lucky when it happens. We are so lucky when we can enjoy the companionship of a child (no longer a child) as between a couple of *people* and not as between the faultfinder and the perennial culprit.

Not, I suppose, as "equals." Those many years' difference is still there, and we are not the same and never can be. But we can have equal dignity, equal privacy, equal rights, and we can laugh at and with each other.

The basis for this wonderful relationship is laid at the start, and it begins, I am very sure indeed, by giving our children their dignity through our own grace and good manners toward them.

We may fail everywhere else, and most of us do fail time and time again, but our children will never hold it against us if we take care not to fail them.

Chapter 16

UN-BIRTHDAYS

IF YOU'RE AN ACTRESS or a baseball player, chances are everybody will find out your age. As Fred Astaire says, "What is this age bit that goes on about actors and athletes, anyway? . . . It's a sort of a newspaper gimmick these days. . . . It amuses me to read it but it also gives me a big fat headache."

I know, Fred, I know. But you don't have to be an actor to get told on. It happens to everybody all the time on the front pages. All you have to do, practically, is dent a fender and something like this will come out in your home-town paper:

> Miss Mary Bartlett, 45, of 1544 Ard Eevin Avenue, Glendale, escaped injury yesterday when her station wagon backed into a beer truck operated by James M. Whorf, 47, an employee of Wilbur Hall Breweries, Inc. Police said...

Police have already said too much. What business of theirs is it that poor Miss Bartlett, a desperate spinster, is on record as forty-five when she has been getting away with thirty-eight for the past eleven years? Mr. Whorf, forty-seven, may not care, but his age isn't news. It would have been news if he had been nine and driving a beer truck.

I say let the police and the city hall reporters shut up about matters that don't concern them.

I tell my age because I can't get out of it. Everybody knows it. If they didn't know, I'd lie, except to the Social Security Administration, by at least twenty years, and I would use a handy figure, like fifty. Or forty-nine.

But turn to page 282 of the 1959 *Information Please Almanac* and there you will find me indecently exposed along with other victims and other theatrical people whose names begin with "B."

Such as: Sidney Blackmer, Vivian Blaine, Ray Bolger, Pat Boone, Richard Boone, Shirley Booth, Victor Borge, Ernest Borgnine, Eddie Bracken, Marlon Brando, Rossano Brazzi, Joe E. Brown, Pamela Brown, Vanessa Brown, Yul Brynner, George Burns, Abe Burrows, Richard Burton, Red Buttons, and Spring Byington.

I want to indorse a campaign started by Dr. Peter J. Steincrohn in his excellent book, *How to Add Years to Your Life*, though I want to subtract, not add, for goodness' sake. The doctor wants to abolish birthdays. He says:

> Your actual age at a given moment depends as much on your philosophy as on your arteries. Yet, do you act your age—or do you act as you feel? You like to believe that you are still young. But, are you allowed to forget that you are growing older? Listen to George Bernard Shaw, who on arriving at his eighty-eighth birthday declared: "To hell with all birthday wishes; I am not celebrating."

The doctor also says:

> With the exception of abject poverty, illness, or death, nothing is more saddening than the realization that the years are slipping by. Life flows on apparently like a gentle, lazy stream, but there is a swift undercurrent which carries us to sea. Do we need birthdays to remind us?

Charles Hanson Towne, an old friend of mine in New York, although he declined to grow old, simply abolished his birthdays, declared them null and void. He called this "Birthday Control."

And Humpty Dumpty and the White Queen coped with the problem years before that by inventing un-birthday presents.

"One can't help growing older," says Alice.

"*One* can't," says Humpty, "but *two* can."

Vasiliv

Which is an intelligent observation. It takes two to
have a birthday: you to have it, and somebody to remind
you of it.

Humpty Dumpty goes on to explain, as you know,
that it is better to celebrate un-birthdays because there
are 364 of them in a year as against only one birthday.

". . . only one for birthday presents, you know.
There's glory for you!"

"I don't know what you mean by glory," says Alice.

"Of course you don't—till I tell you. I mean 'there's
a nice knockdown argument for you.' "

Alice, by the way, was seven years and six months old, according to her friend Lewis Carroll. I have a friend who insists that I am the same age as Alice, a statement which can be taken two ways and I'm not sure I like either one. Alice would be almost a hundred today.

Why we Americans put so much emphasis on age—and what I really mean is youth—I don't know. It's because, I suppose, we consider ourselves a young country. Europeans make no such false emphasis and men and women with a great many birthdays don't find it necessary to apologize for being attractive. One example is enough. Maurice Chevalier.

And now the British, or at least their newspaper reporters, have succumbed to the American urge to deplore anything except callow youth. I refer, of course, to the recent press uproar in London when Miss Ginger Rogers came to town. There was a great outcry in headlines because the English discovered that Ginger was forty-seven—as fresh and crisp as ever, as gay and light and charming as ever—but forty-seven! You'd think they thought she was Grandma Moses, or Whistler's mother, looking young under false pretenses. Forty-seven is nothing at all, nor is any age unless you're a cheese, but I wish Ginger had had the foresight to start lying at least thirty years ago. I wish I had.

Let's all set ourselves back at least ten or fifteen years NOW—and have no more birthdays. The only birthday that counts, you know, is the first one, the day you arrived, and that was happily celebrated by your parents and your father's friends who smoked cigars.

What depressed me most about my accumulation of years were the milestone decades. Twenty was a frothy ball, of course. But thirty was a despair and a threat, a morbid reminder that I was "getting on," was grown up, was responsible, was no longer "a girl." Twenty-nine, mind you, was not sad, nor was thirty-one. It's those decade signposts that jar us so. I know a man now past sixty, a brilliant fellow, who tells me that his thirtieth birthday was the most desperate day of his life. He hadn't got very far in his profession, he thought he had wasted his time, made too many mistakes, frittered away his life. He was a slow starter, as it turned out, and didn't begin to hit his quick, far-going stride until he was almost forty-five. But at thirty he thought he was a failure—merely because it was his birthday.

Forty, I imagine, is the hardest milestone for a woman. It was for me. I thought I was done up, tucked away, wrapped in a shawl, hot-water-bottled, and filed in the archives. I wouldn't have felt that way if I hadn't known I was forty on a particular day.

I mentioned Fred Astaire, who is always a delight to mention. The press made a great thing recently about his age, called him "the aging Fred Astaire," the "durable Fred," such things as that, always pointing up that Fred was about to be sixty years old. Then, just a few days before his birthday (which he ignored) he won nine Emmy awards for his fine television show, *An Evening with Fred Astaire*. In that same year he went to Australia to become a dramatic actor in *On the Beach*. And he wrote a book. Sixty? Not in muscle, mind, or viewpoint. This boy is ageless and has more un-birthdays before him than anybody I know. Let's call his next show *A Morning with Fred Astaire*.

I know a remarkable lady, a great-grandmother, whose true age is eighty-one. She doesn't know I know her age and I'd forget it, too, except that when I see her step out, erect, supple, walking like a young major, I become envious of her and recall her years. She goes to concerts, works for the USO, and plays a rugged game of contract bridge. It took a bit of doing and tact, but I finally worked around to the question I wanted to ask her: "How do you keep so young?"

She was baffled for an answer at first. The matter of age had not occurred to her.

"I suppose," she finally offered, "you might say it's because *I go with younger people*. They are twenty or thirty years younger than I am, but they don't know it. They think I'm their contemporary. I don't lie about my age—I just don't tell it. So it may be that they keep me young and going. It's how they treat me that seems to count.

"Why be embarrassed by birthdays? They're only for children and George Washington."

My own birthday is August 6, in case you're curious, and the year of my advent was 1886. But I hereby declare both dates out of order. From now on it's un-birthdays for me.

Chapter 17

WHEN TO TELL YOUR AGE

As I LOOK about me I see that some of my unfortunate friends have grown older, although they haven't aged at the same rate, like bottles in a wine cellar. Some who were older than I was forty years ago are now younger than I am. And some who had many years the gift of youth on me are now older.

Age, of course, is not a matter of years but a matter of spirit, good health, good fortune, how old other people think you are, and how much you are willing to tell.

Most of my friends have had ups and downs (with the exception of an English comedian who insists that for him life goes sideways). Some have made and lost fortunes. A few, luckier or wiser, are as rich as the dickens. But rich, poor or just "comfortable," their so-called age has a lot to do with their activity. Or their activity has had a lot to do with their age.

At any rate, I'm told getting older is now a national problem. People are living longer and staying young longer. Life expectancy has increased so hugely that today 12 per cent of the population of this country is over sixty-five—and, because uninformed employers think that sixty-five is "old," many of the 12 per cent are unhappily out of work.

I don't get this kind of information from notes I made up and stuck behind pictures in my sitting room. I learned about the increasing age rate from my friend Johnnie Johnson, manager of the Social Security office in Santa Monica. Mr. Johnson tells me stories and gives me money.

I didn't know I was eligible for the money, I didn't know I had money coming to me that was mine, earned, paid up, there for me to collect, not a dole, not a handout, and not charity. Indeed, I was overdue and I got, in addition to my monthly stipend, a small back payment. I imagine many other women may not know what may be due to them or what they have to look forward to.

You don't have to be broke to get your Social Security

old age insurance. You can have other income and you don't have to retire.

Take Eddie Cantor, who was first starred by Flo Ziegfeld, and who is of course a man of very considerable means. Eddie resisted quitting, even after a coronary thrombosis. "To retire is to die a little," he said. He never would have applied for his benefits, and stood to lose a good deal of money by not applying, if he hadn't been told that he could "partially retire." He earns large sums when he works, but like all people in show business, including the stars, he is often between parts. But so long as he doesn't earn more than $1200 a year he can receive benefits from Social Security every month. It doesn't take Eddie Cantor long to make $1200, but even so he still gets benefits for any month in which he doesn't earn more than $100.

Eddie, who calls himself the "schnorrer," a Yiddish word that means "beggar," has raised millions and millions of dollars for other people by campaigning, asking, and pleading for it. It hadn't occurred to him that he could ask anything for himself. He was staggered when he discovered that he was eligible.

The trouble is, most people don't ask. Eddie asked, then appeared on a weekly fifteen-minute television show, *Social Security in Action*, here in Hollywood. He explained Social Security exactly the way Ed Kramer, manager of the Hollywood office, had explained it to him:

"I've paid my Social Security taxes for twenty-two years," Eddie said. "And now I'm sixty-five. So I'm drawing my benefits just as I would from any other insurance policy I'd paid on. Sure, I don't need the money. Social Security isn't charity. It's based on the amount of work you've done and the taxes you've paid."

A great many people, many of them showfolks, learned about Social Security through that program. And this show isn't a giveaway program, either. It's merely a reminder, like a dramatized bank statement, that you paid the government something and *for once* you can get it back.

E. Wolfe Gilbert, who wrote *Ramona* and *Waiting for the Robert E. Lee*, filed his claim because he heard Cantor. "Wolfie" is over seventy-two. He has a daughter under eighteen and a wife considerably younger than sixty-two. Under the rules, he can draw his checks without any restrictions because he is past seventy-two. His Social Security is an annuity for him, and his wife and daughter also receive benefits each month.

Eddie Cantor told me that he was in a Beverly Hills barbershop having a shave just after the newspapers had shown him getting his first Social Security check. Someone lifted the hot towel on his face and kissed him.

"Ha! I knew I was beautiful, but well—!" Eddie said, popping his platter-sized eyes at the barber.

But his kisser was Chico Marx. "That was for telling me about Social Security," Chico said.

A good many other Hollywood people, like me, are drawing their Social Security—meantime working and keeping young by keeping active. Marjorie Rambeau (she's still beautiful), Grandma Reynolds, Charles ("Cap'n Andy" of *Show Boat*) Winninger, Frank Orth and his lovely wife, Ann Codee, come to mind, and many more. The late Jimmie Gleason and the late Cecil B. De Mille both appeared on the television program, *Social Security in Action*. Jimmie said he was "proud to claim his Social Security," while Mr. De Mille described Social Security as "living insurance."

So, if you've been holding back from false pride—or ignorance—pray discard the false pride and go see your Social Security manager as I did. He may put money in the bank for you. Also, he may keep you from having trouble with the law because of your housekeeper. I'll come to that.

My point is, of course, that all these Social Security stars are still *active*. They still consider themselves young. Take Francis X. Bushman, who's been around long enough to be old but isn't—you ought to see him in person, the handsome devil. He says, "Here I am, seventy-six, ready and able to work, and the director hires a forty-year-old actor to play a seventy-eight-year-old man! I guess I was too young for the part."

It's a sad fact that in movies and television, as in other industries, some executives are afraid to employ older people. Producers think the oldsters will "blow their lines." It's the young and inexperienced who blow, not us. You should hear "old" Clem Bevans read lines by the page, without hesitation.

So, to add to our conversations about getting on with the years gracefully (make it "forgetting on with the years"?), let me suggest that you find out about your Social Security.

Of course, if you've always lied about your age, as so many women have—and why not?—you'll have to dig up proof of your birth date. You'll find that the Social Security people are helpful there. It may take a spell, but aside from birth certificates (I have none), they can accept baptismal records (mine are in London), family Bibles, religious papers, applications for insurance policies, club membership applications, property deeds, and voting registrations. The only thing required is that the proof be old enough to have legal validity. Language is no barrier. They'll translate.

Here's an odd one: The SS people accepted proof of one woman's age because it had been made on an original Currier & Ives print, which certainly dated *her*. In another case, Ed Kramer tells me, a sinewy old man couldn't produce paperwork of any kind to prove his age. He did prove it, though, by removing a door from an old farmhouse and lugging that in as a document. His name and date of birth were carved in the thick oak, which was obviously ancient. Aged in the wood, perhaps. Don't print your age on old doors unless you want people to find out how old you are.

Igor Stravinsky, the composer (*Firebird Suite* and *Rite of Spring*), had less trouble but his documentation was more interesting. He produced an Imperial Russian passport which he'd used in all the countries of Europe before World War I. To accommodate all his visas the document had been patched and added to until it was two feet wide and five feet long—very thorough proof that Igor was seventy-seven years old. The only trouble was that, like me and so many of my friends, he had lost money by not knowing about Social Security soon enough.

He learned from his housekeeper. They were discussing the tax on her wages, which inspired her to ask if he had applied for his own benefits. Stravinsky was amused, then curious. He wrote a letter to find out—and found out that he could have been receiving benefits for four years. He and his wife lost $5,000 by being tardy.

Speaking of housekeepers—as if everybody had one, but you may be one of the blessed—I used to have a woman who came in one day a week. She objected when

I suggested that I deduct the SS tax from her pay. She said she didn't want a check because it was hard for her to cash. She added that her husband was under Social Security and she'd get a wife's share eventually, so why bother? I thought that was reasonable enough until it was explained to me how wrong I was.

My one-day-a-week housekeeper had two children under eighteen. If she had died, benefits would have been paid to the children—if she had paid the small tax. Worst of all, ignoring the tax could have cost me, and may still cost me. It's like this: A woman can collect her own social security when she is past sixty-two, can't get her wife's payments unless her husband is sixty-five. So, one day this ex-worker of mine could waltz into a Social Security office and announce:

"I worked for Miss Burke in 1957 and she didn't take any tax out of my pay."

Then a nice young man would call on me to see if this was true. Then the Director of Internal Revenue would send me a bill for my share of the tax, her share of the tax, interest, and penalties.

You'd better be aware of this. If anyone works for you, investigate, find out what to do, and pay. This applies to maids, housekeepers, cooks, and chauffeurs. And a good thing. Jimmy Durante, for instance, has a housekeeper who's worked for him many years. She'll be able to draw her full Social Security benefit when she retires.

You can realize how important this is when you consider the number of women who have toiled all their lives as domestics, never being able to have any sort of pension or retirement plan.

So, if you are a housekeeper, maid, or cook (bless your heart, I wish I knew you!) there is a retirement plan for you. Take care to do your part.

Another reason why all women should want to be covered by Social Security, even if their husbands are making a lot of money, is the disability part of the law. If you become handicapped so that you can't do any kind of work, the benefits start when you are fifty, not sixty-two. The requirement is that you must have worked under SS at least half of the ten years before your disability. And even if you aren't fifty, your record will be "blocked" at the date you became disabled. When you are old enough to collect, your benefits will be based on earnings during your healthy and working life.

Social Security benefits can be paid to you on your own account or on your husband's account as his wife. You can draw your benefits on your own account any time after you are sixty-two, but if you make your claim before you are sixty-five your check will be reduced in return for getting it sooner. If you are drawing a wife's benefit you can get it when you are sixty-two if your husband is sixty-five and has qualified for his benefits. If you are a widow you can get your widow's benefit at sixty-two without any reductions.

If you are a young mother with children under eighteen, and your husband should die, you would get a death payment varying between $99 and $255, depending upon the amount of benefits he had earned. Then you would get monthly payments for yourself and your children. Depending on your husband's earnings and the number of children you have, this could come to as much as $254 a month. As you can see, I've become very interested in this Social Security thing because so many of my friends are getting returns from it in one way or another. Some are retired actors and actresses who you'd never guess could be old enough to qualify; another is a young widow of a friend of mine; and, of course, I'm getting benefits myself. Because I'm over seventy-two I can draw my benefits even though I may do roles in movies or in television for wages and even though my publisher pays me for this book as a self-employed person. As Cantor says, "Social Security is not charity—it's paid because you earned it."

One of the chief criticisms of Social Security is, "I get my Social Security but it is not enough to live on." Social Security was never intended to be enough to live on. It is hoped that people will have other resources—income from property or investments or pension or retirement plans, from former employment. Of course, this isn't always true and many people have nothing to fall back on but their Social Security. And if as they say it isn't enough to live on, I'll have to agree with them. These people can then ask for another part of Social Security called Old Age Assistance. I don't know much about this except that it is different in every state, and applicants have to show need in order to qualify for it. If they are already getting Social Security old age benefits from the Federal Government, the amount they are getting is income and the state will pay the difference between their assistance amount and their Social Security check. So, if you are one of those whose Social Security check is not enough, get in touch with the Bureau of Public Assistance in your state to see if you can qualify for State Old Age Assistance, too.

As Will Rogers used to say, "All I know is what I read in the papers." So far as Social Security is concerned, all I know is what Johnnie Johnson told me when I made my claim in Santa Monica, and what I've read in a little government booklet, *Your Social Security*. You can read it, too. Any Social Security office will send it to you, free of charge, if you phone in and ask for it.

And if you'll tell your age. I know a story about that, too. One of my dear friends, whose name I won't tell you, always lied about her age. She would have lied to me except that I knew her when. She was actually years older than her husband, who promptly claimed his Social Security when he became sixty-five.

He waited until he figured that she too was sixty-five, then took her in to file her claim. My poor friend was beside herself but still a good liar. She filled in all the forms with the age she'd given her husband, and was doing fine until the young man at the desk asked for proof.

At this point she thought desperately fast and sent her husband out to the car to look for a nonexistent family Bible. When he was gone, she told SS the truth, signed another application and produced her true birth certificate. These papers the Social Security man hid in a desk drawer when the husband returned. He didn't tell on her. And she got the money.

It turns out, she discovered, that interviews and statements to the Social Security people are absolutely confidential. Only three people in the world know that woman's age: She knows it, I know it, and the discreet young man behind the desk knows it.

I guess this is the only place in the world where it pays a woman to tell the truth about her age.

Chapter 18

OUT OF MY HEAD

THERE IS NO FEAST so delicious as the burned toast and peculiar coffee served by a husband to a wife as breakfast in bed.

* * *

Men are such poor risks. They will offer up their lives for love, money, sex, power, patriotism, or a weekend of golf. Women avoid dying for golf.

* * *

Some of the happiest, most worth-while women in the world are spinsters—Old Maids. They can be the

best friends boys, girls, young men, ever have. They fulfill themselves as mothers. It is impossible for an old bachelor to feel like a father.

* * *

The supreme quality in women is graciousness. A woman can be as plain as a board or as fat as a tub and still be outstanding, and attractive to men, if she knows how to be gracious.

* * *

Many a shaky marriage could be saved by a hot breakfast—in a hotel.

* * *

I never knew a rich woman who owned a cat.

* * *

I firmly believe, from observation, that the death of both parents harms a child less than a divorce.

* * *

Noel Coward says that certain women should be struck regularly, like gongs. Mr. Coward is unmarried.

* * *

Advice to boys and girls: Young women, be brave; young men, be kind.

* * *

Enjoy the moment, this moment, now, with your children. Think about it. "Sit on your own shoulder" and watch yourself enjoy it so you can always remember. They will be gone so very soon.

* * *

Listen to the old. They may not be more intelligent than you are. They may be downright ignorant. They may give all the wrong reasons, and they may be testy. But they are often right.

* * *

Go to church. You may believe nothing. But at least once a week you can join, if only in silent communication, a lot of hopeful people trying to learn good will.

* * *

Marriage is still woman's chief aim and business in life. This is easy to prove. Look at the many excellent mass-circulation magazines edited specifically to teach women marriage. There are no such magazines for men.

* * *

It's no surprise to me that Communism has produced no heroines or female saints and prophets. Women are much too practical to believe in Communism. When a woman claims to be a Communist, she is following some man.

* * *

There's a lot of nonsense written about how money won't buy happiness. Well, I've had a lot of money and a lot of unhappiness at the same time. And I've been poor and happy. But the most fun of all was being happy *and* having money.

* * *

So many people don't know how to say "Thank you." They think there is some mystic protocol, some formula. You don't have to consult a book of rules. Just say it.

* * *

The most difficult three words for a married man are "I love you." Wives pout because their husbands don't say those words to them every day. Men should say them, but they think it's unnecessary, think they have proved their love. But there are some women who'd rather hear it than know it.

* * *

I never was "like a sister" to any man. And neither was any other woman except a sister.

* * *

It isn't gray hair or a crick in the neck that tells a woman she's "getting on." She knows it the first time her hostess gives her a dinner partner obviously much too old for her.

* * *

A woman isn't as old as she thinks she is. She's as old as men think she is.

* * *

I never knew a woman who could tell a risqué story effectively. Women may think sex is fun, but only men ever think it is funny.

* * *

According to Dr. Popenoe, and every instance I can think of, a difference in ages—either way—is the most negligible of all handicaps to a happy marriage.

* * *

Plea from all women to all men: We'll powder our noses at least twenty times a day; please shave at least once.

* * *

I thought I knew the Lord's Prayer, but it turned out I didn't. I wonder how many people do know it well enough to quote it correctly.

Note the punctuation and capital letters:

Our Father, who are in heaven, Hallowed be thy Name. Thy kingdom come. Thy will be done, On earth as it is in heaven. Give us this day our daily bread. And forgive us our trespasses, As we forgive those who trespass against us. And lead us not into temptation, But deliver us from evil. For thine is the kingdom, and the power, and the glory, for ever and ever. Amen.

Challenge your children, perhaps your friends, on this. It's at least one way to make them, and us, say a prayer.

Chapter 19

HOW TO WRITE A BOOK
WITH BILLIE BURKE
by Cameron Shipp

ON WEDNESDAY NIGHT, January 28, 1959, after the curtain had fallen on the last act of *Listen to the Mocking Bird* by Edward Chodorov, the Shubert Theater in Washington, D.C., caught fire and was destroyed. Miss Billie Burke, Miss Eva Le Gallienne, and Miss Una Merkel, stars of the play, were safely in their hotel rooms when the blaze started. If they had been on stage or in their dressing rooms, which were two flights up and reached by narrow iron stairways, they would almost certainly have been burned to death. The ladies thanked Providential timing for saving them, but the fire in the theater was a professional disaster. The sets and the scenery were a total loss and *Listen to the Mocking Bird* was not able to reopen. Miss Burke was particularly distressed. There had been good hope that the play would reach Broadway, where she had not appeared since 1944, in *Mrs. January and Mr. X* by her friend the late Zoë Akins. She was eager to return to the street of many past triumphs—twenty-one plays—after years of work in Hollywood. And in *Listen to the Mocking Bird*, which was a drama, she thought that she might at long last demonstrate that she could solve and portray a character much deeper than those she once described as the "twitter-pated, bird-witted ladies" she had been compelled to play in motion pictures. Her Broadway plays, although they were all comedies, were highly sophisticated plays, much superior to her Hollywood material. It has always been known that her range was wide. But Hollywood, which is essentially a manufacturing center turning out nationally advertised and packaged products, stuck to a salable commodity in Miss Burke's nonsense parts and gave her nothing else to do.

After the fire Miss Burke returned unhappily to California and to her surprise discovered that Warner Bros. Studio wanted her for *The Young Philadelphians*, and in a dramatic, not a comedy part. She threw herself into this, liking her role immensely, she said, "Because this woman I do gets down to brass tacks. She's smart. I used some people I know in creating her." *Time* magazine, in reviewing the film recently, noted in regard to Miss Burke that "the lady is a thief," which is to say that she stole the show. Prophets in Hollywood quickly forecast that she would be nominated for an Academy Award. And she found time to work on this book, an undertaking close to her heart for which she had been preparing for ten years by writing notes in pencil on yellow scratchpads and essays in green ink on embossed letterheads. She tucked these away behind pictures and under seat cushions. Some she left on her desk where they were never seen again. All told she lost thousands of words, which she bemoans as a considerable loss to literature.

With a book and a motion picture to make at the same time, Miss Burke wasted no time regretting the destruction of the Shubert. She was calm about the incident and inclined to dismiss getting a theater burned out from under her as something that was bound to happen to everybody now and then. Her chief interest in the matter was an amber-colored cat.

The cat was a member of the cast, called "Tabatha" in the play but later renamed "Tommy" when he revealed himself as a male. He had a good part, and his pretended demise by poison hinged one of the dramatic developments of the show. He worked with Miss Burke, a cat lover from away back, who took curtain calls with him and had him wave a paw to the audience. When the show closed, its producers proposed to dispose humanely of Tommy, but Miss Burke, in horror, snatched him away and brought him home by plane. He is now established on a bed on a side table in her dining room, which is magnificently furnished with Ziegfeldian pieces, and is amiable, though distant, with three elderly Burke cats called Bibby, Bandy, and Sunny Jim.

"I want to do a chapter about cats," Miss Burke said one day as work began on her book, "several chapters. Please remind me to put in something about cats—you know, in an appropriate place." Soon after that, she found her notes about mothers-in-law, which excited her, and the cats, to her regret, got lost.

Miss Burke also had, she said, a good many thousand words about love, a subject which she approves mightily, but most of these had become scattered between her sitting room, her drawing room, and her kitchen. "At any rate," she said, "I want to be sure to put in something nice about love."

Her favorite method of communication, however, is not note-making. She prefers Western Union above all else and next to that the telephone. Any friend of hers is likely to get two or three long telegrams a day from her, not necessarily containing news. She sends them as tokens of affection with warm expressions of love and blessings. Undoubtedly she acquired the telegram habit from Flo Ziegfeld, who used to send dozens a day, often to people in his own theater, only a few feet from him. Mr. Ziegfeld's telegrams were frequently stern orders or bitter complaints that his press agents were working to keep him anonymous. Miss Burke's are, of course, a sheer delight.

She keeps a bulging and battered leather notebook jampacked with names and addresses of friends and calls them up, no matter where they are. She is at her warm and funny best by long distance. The vice-president of her publishing house recently fell under the Burke telephonic charm, which was expressed three or four times a week, California to New York, in conversations which lasted thirty or forty minutes. "How can you afford all those long distance tolls?" a friend remonstrated.

"Oh *that*," said Miss Burke. "That's a mere nothing. Besides, I have discovered that you can call your publisher collect."

Her address book, which she takes with her wherever she travels, contains treasures other than names and addresses. She uses it as a scrapbook, sticking in numerous clippings and copies of favorite poems. She loses the notebook regularly and is in despair until she finds it. About a year ago she misplaced it somewhere in Beverly Hills. She was delighted when a lady called from downtown Los Angeles to say she had it and wanted to return it to Billie Burke in person. The lady was calling from a bar, where she proposed that Miss Burke meet her. Miss

Burke did, and spent four hours in the bar happily discussing poetry. She was surprised, later, when her family scolded her and told her she might have been in danger and that, at any rate, a bar was not her style. "Why, it was delightful," Miss Burke said, "and besides, I could have handled the situation if necessary."

Since she reads a great deal (in French as well as in English), and usually copies down or clips whatever she likes, Miss Burke has virtually compiled an anthology in her scrap-address book. Some of her favorite lines are these:

> Earth's crammed with Heaven
> And every common bush afire with God.
> —Elizabeth Barrett Browning

> Dear Lord, let us recount to Thee
> Some of the great things Thou hast done for me,
> Thy little one.
> —Christina Rosetti

And these lines, from B. Cooksley, which she proposes eventually to have inscribed on the Florenz Ziegfeld crypt in Forest Lawn:

> He wore the crown he'd searched life through
> at last he drained the cup and found
> the heartache and the rue more sweeter on the
> travel up.

Like many another actor and actress who has created an image on screen, and has performed the image in public for many years, Billie Burke often reverts in private to typecasting. She has played comic parts in motion pictures so long (her vague, fluttering ladies) that she goes in and out of character, anywhere, without difficulty. People who do not know her well find it hard to tell whether she is being funny in a conditioned reflex or being funny because she thinks people think she ought to be funny. Let's clear up that illusion. The lady knows what she is doing at all times. She knows what *non sequiturs* are and thoroughly enjoys dropping them for other people to trip over. She looks on her own work with a clear professional eye. She is forthright, astute, and precise when she wants to be. But she is capable of saying, "It doesn't make any difference what I mean, you know what I say," and of leaving the matter there if you don't get the point.

"I imagine some of this will be a funny book," she said one day. "It will almost have to be because I want to say some things that are true, and to say them all of a sudden. If you do that, you usually create an effect of shock, the truth being such a rare thing. People are appalled by it and don't know what to do except to laugh."

Miss Burke's truths were assembled in interviews, by telephone, and by having her read her notes, and expand them, into a tape recorder. She tried at first to manage a recorder herself but without success. She claimed that the machine was a monster and that the tapes got loose and swirled around the room and tripped her up. But when someone else was on hand to start and stop the recorder, she was delighted. At her first session, she talked rapidly for two hours without stopping—clearly and emphatically, like an actress on stage who knew her lines cold. She was disappointed when evening fell and the recorder was taken away from her. Subsequently, she taped thousands of more words, most of which appear in this book. She had only one failure. Carried away one afternoon with admiration for soap, she spoke three thousand words on how to take a bath.

One other section of Miss Burke's prose is also missing, with the apologies of her collaborator. She wrote with great care a long tribute to Sears Roebuck, a corporation she admires because "they have so many pretty, useful things for sale, and so cheap." Miss Burke was disappointed when that did not become a chapter. But here is the tribute: Billie Burke likes Sears Roebuck.

Shortly after this book was completed, and, indeed, while Coward-McCann, Inc., was starting to put it in type, Miss Burke—now in full flight of authorship—was still searching for notes she was sure she had put somewhere. She had not, for instance, listed her favorite actresses, but these were easy to remember: Katharine Cornell, whom she considers the most glamorous, the most "theater," of all; Helen Hayes, Ethel Barrymore, Mrs. Minnie Maddern Fiske, Ruth Gordon, and Siobhan McKenna.

As for actors, she stopped firmly with the name of John Drew, her leading man in her first American play, and declined to go further. "He brushed his hair so beautifully," she said.

"And be sure," she said, "to sum it all up with this advice: 'Girls, keep your shine coming from within and powder on your nose, and life will be much more fun.' "

Miss Burke paused for a moment and said she had one more suggestion. "I think somewhere in this book we ought to say something about women," she said.